❖ DOS CAMINOS ❖

TACOS

RECIPES FOR EVERYONE'S FAVORITE MEXICAN STREET FOOD

IVY STARK with Joanna Pruess

DOS CAMINOS TACOS

DOS CAMINOS TACOS

Recipes for Everyone's Favorite Mexican Street Food

IVY STARK with Joanna Pruess

Also by IVY STARK with Joanna Pruess
Dos Caminos Mexican Street Food

Photography:

All photography by Noah Feckman unless otherwise indicated

Photographs printed with permission of BR Guest: pages 12, 13,
16, 45, 270.

Photographs © Shutterstock: pages 19, 20, 21, 26, 35, 40, 93, 169,
189, 203, 249, 258-261, 265, 267

Published by The Countryman Press,
P.O. Box 748, Woodstock, VT 05091

Distributed by W. W. Norton & Company, Inc., 500 Fifth Avenue,
New York, NY 10110
Printed in the United States by Versa Press, Peoria, Illinois

10 9 8 7 6 5 4 3 2 1

◆◆◆◆◆◆◆◆◆◆◆◆◆◆◆◆◆◆◆◆

To the borough of Brooklyn where I live:

The place I love most on earth for its inspiring diversity of people,
neighborhoods, great food,
appreciation of innovation, and resilience.

◆◆◆◆◆◆◆◆◆◆◆◆◆◆◆

CONTENTS

DOS CAMINOS TACOS

INTRODUCTION

WE SERVE THOUSANDS AND THOUSANDS OF TACOS EACH WEEK AT DOS CAMINOS, AND OCCASIONALLY A GUEST ASKS ABOUT THEIR ORIGINS.

Having majored in history in college, and traveled and cooked throughout Mexico for decades, I still don't have a conclusive answer. Although Mexicans have eaten corn tortillas with meat, insects, vegetables, or beans folded inside them for centuries, it wasn't until the 20th century that the taco achieved its current popularity.

One theory is that 18th-century silver miners called the small charges they used to excavate ore "tacos," referring to little pieces of paper wrapped around gunpowder that were stuck into the mountains and detonated, writes Mexican food scholar Jeffrey Pilcher in *Smithsonian* magazine. They were first mentioned in print at the end of the 19th century, and this included a reference to *tacos de minero,* or miner's tacos.

Whether these origins are fact or fiction is unknown. But by extension, the mildly spicy or fiery dishes might be thought of as explosive in the mouth.

Once Mexicans crossed the Rio Grande into Texas—still part of New Spain at the time—tacos became a staple of southwestern or Tex-Mex cooking. By the mid-20th century, they had become mainstream in American cuisine and indispensable items in supermarkets and fast-food franchises.

I have a taco notebook that grows fatter and fatter every year. It's stained with salsa and greasy fingerprints, crinkled from splashes of beer and *agua fresca,* and positively stuffed with menus, place mats, matchbooks, photos, and scribbled recipes from the many *taquerías* I have visited in search of the perfect taco . . . and I have found some stellar ones.

Everyone has personal favorites. Californians are particularly passionate about their tacos and are lucky enough to live in

a place full of great *taquerías* and trucks, but I will throw mine out here in no particular order:

In Mexico City, **El Villamelón** for their "Campechanos" made with a combination of *cecina* (salted and dried meat), *longaniza* (spicy sausage), and *chicharrón* (crispy pork rind), and the guy who sells the amazing meringues just outside Los Panchos, in the Polanco neighborhood, for his *carnitas.* **Beatricita** for tacos *guisados*—a stew over a tortilla that's a DF (Federal District of Mexico City) thing. In Puebla, **Las Ranas** for the tacos *arabes,* and **Tacos Tony** for tacos

al pastor. And in Baja, **Tacos la Floresta** for expert fish tacos.

In Los Angeles, I practically lived on tacos in my college days and I would drive all the way across town from my apartment in Venice to **Los Cinco Puntos** for their tongue tacos. These days, I head to the ball fields in Red Hook on the weekend for **Chai Perez' Piaztlan Authentic Mexican Food Truck** and her goat *barbacoa.* I'm always on the lookout for great tacos.

Today Americans are obsessed with tacos, seeking out the most authentic versions in traditional *taquerías* and having fun with the creative versions American chefs are endlessly playing with. Regardless of their origins, a taco with a wonderfully seasoned filling in a warm, handmade corn tortilla is an exquisite thing!

I think the tacos that our restaurants serve reflect our name Dos Caminos, or two roads. For the most part, they are prepared according to traditional recipes, many of which have been around for centuries. Sometimes, however, I veer off that main path and try a somewhat modern or more creative approach. But when making these decisions, I always try to respect the origins of the whole taco experience.

In this book, you'll find some of the most popular tacos served at our restaurants, as well as some that I have prepared for holidays and other special events. I hope you enjoy your discovery of the many possible varieties of tacos and that these will inspire you to create some of your own.

WHAT MAKES A TACO

The key to a great taco is the **tortillas**, the flatbreads that are the center of every Mexican meal. I can't emphasize how much better a homemade tortilla tastes and even feels in your mouth compared with those that are commercially produced. Try making them at least once. I think you'll be amazed how easy they are.

Most tacos in this book and across Mexico are made with soft corn tortillas of white, blue, or yellow cornmeal. Corn, treated with an alkaline solution before being ground into flour, had been used for millennia before the Spaniards introduced wheat into the country. The cornmeal is then mixed with water and made into balls of *masa,* or dough, that are flattened on a tortilla press and then cooked on a *comal.*

The major exceptions to corn tortillas are in Baja California, where their fish tacos are traditionally wrapped in flour tortillas, and U.S. border states where flour tortillas were created using local white flour. While not the original, homemade flour tortillas can be quite delicious.

Generally we use tortillas that are between 4 and 6 inches in diameter in the restaurants. In this book, unless otherwise specified, 5- to 6-inch tacos are fine. Contrary to packaged taco shells in supermarkets, rarely are tortillas fried. Most often they are just heated until soft and served warm.

For the **filling**, technically almost anything can be used, and there are countless creative taco interpretations by today's chefs. That said, Mexicans always have tortillas on the table, so whatever they're eating, from meat loaf to grilled fish or vegetables, grilled fish or vegetables, can become a taco. (Check out my recipe for Isthmian-Style Meat Loaf Tacos on page 210.)

Salsas are another essential component of tacos. They can be as familiar as *Pico de Gallo* and *Salsa Verde Cruda,* two of the most commonly used sauces found in every *taquería.* Neither would be inappropriate to add except on dessert tacos. Another very popular sauce is made with *chiles de árbol,* spicier, fiery red chiles. Throughout this book, however, you'll find numerous other choices. Look at the recipes and mix and match at will.

Finally, bite for bite, **garnishes and side dishes** often bring the whole taco experience together. In most recipes, I suggest salsa, garnishes, and side dishes, but I hope you will explore the diverse choices throughout this book. Some taco recipes are as flexible as you want them to be: Make the filling and add whichever salsa and toppings appeal to you. In others, I have suggested some of my favorite garnishes. But I hate rules when it comes to recipes. Have fun with your tacos!

I've tried to share some of the satisfying and diverse possibilities—both traditional and creative—that tacos can add to your cooking experiences. I hope you'll share them with your family and friends.

—Ivy Stark

A FEW GENERAL NOTES ◆◆◆◆◆◆◆◆◆◆◆◆◆◆◆◆◆◆◆◆◆◆◆◆◆◆

INGREDIENTS

OIL: I usually use "blended" oil: a combination of 90 percent vegetable (canola) oil mixed with 10 percent olive oil. This way, you get oil with the olive flavor but with a much higher flame point. Unless a recipe specifies "olive oil," use blended oil.

ONIONS: In Mexico, white onions are most commonly used in cooking. However, yellow onions are fine.

SALT: I prefer either fine or coarse sea salt or kosher salt. To me, iodized salt imparts a metallic taste to food.

If you come upon an ingredient that you don't understand, you'll find it in the back of this book.

QUANTITIES: Throughout the recipes, in most cases I've tried to specify quantities for salsas, condiments, and side dishes. However, these are broad guidelines. Please enjoy your tacos *your* way. If you like more or less salsa, fine. If you want to use other condiments: also fine. My recipes are only meant as guidelines. As a point of reference, if you want to eyeball amounts of filling, at the restaurants we usually put about $1/3$ cup or 3 ounces of protein in each taco.

SPECIAL EQUIPMENT: Very little special equipment is needed to make tacos, and you probably already have most of it in your kitchen. A cast-iron skillet or *plancha*, electric blender, and food processor are very helpful. A barbecue is useful for grilling. For authentic Mexican cooking, a tortilla press and a *comal,* flat griddle, also are helpful.

TECHNIQUES

GARLIC CLOVES, ROASTED: Set a heavy ungreased skillet or griddle over medium heat. Roast the garlic cloves, turning frequently, until blackened in spots and very soft, 10 to 15 minutes.

TORTILLAS, WARMED: Wrap the tortillas in foil and put them in a preheated 350-degree oven or toaster oven for 10 minutes. Or place them directly on the griddle or grill and cook until lightly browned on each side, about 1 minute, turning once.

TORTILLAS, FRIED: In a heavy skillet, heat about ½ cup of blended oil to 350 degrees or until a drop of water added to the pan pops. Using tongs, slide the tortillas into the oil and quickly cook until small brown spots form on one side, 10 to 20 seconds. Turn and cook the second side to color. Remove to paper towels to blot the oil. You can stack fried tortillas on top of one another, separated by paper towels.

CHILES, ROASTING (FRESH): To enhance the flavor of chiles and remove their thin outer skin, put them directly over medium heat on a gas stovetop to char the flesh. Turn them often until the flesh is evenly blistered, about 5 to 10 minutes, depending on size. Do not let them burn.

Transfer to a plastic bag and close, or cover with a damp cloth, and let them cool for 10 to 15 minutes. Using your hands or under cold running water, slide the skins off. If any skin sticks, use a sharp paring knife. Make a lengthwise cut along the chile, remove the seeds and membranes, and dice.

CHILES, ROASTING AND REHYDRATING (DRIED): To enhance the aroma and make dried chiles easier to grind or puree, first wipe them and discard the stem. Slit one long side to remove the seeds and veins. Lightly roast the chiles in a preheated heavy skillet or griddle over medium heat until you smell a toasty aroma, 2 to 3 minutes, pressing them flat with a metal spatula to cook them evenly, and taking care not to burn them.

Transfer the chiles to a bowl, add just enough lukewarm water to cover completely, and soak until soft and pliable, 5 to 10 minutes, stirring occasionally to rehydrate evenly. Drain, reserving some of the soaking liquid, and puree in the jar of an electric blender, adding a little of the rehydrating liquid, if needed, so the blades turn easily. If desired, strain to remove any bits of skin.

SPICES, TOASTED: In a skillet over medium-high heat, toast whole spices for 2 to 4 minutes, shaking the pan often to make sure they don't burn. Use in dishes either whole or ground to enliven their flavor and fragrance.

TOMATOES, ROASTED: Toss tomatoes with a little blended oil, and season with salt and pepper. Place them uncut in a heavy skillet or on a cookie sheet lined with aluminum foil. Cook over high heat on top of the stove or in a hot oven in a single layer until the skins are blistered and browned, shaking the pan and turning occasionally. They can also be cooked under a broiler.

TORTILLAS, SALSA, AND CONDIMENTS

Basics

BASIC TORTILLA
Masa

YIELD: 12-16 TORTILLAS, DEPENDING ON SIZE

At the center of any Mexican meal are corn tortillas.
They are quick and easy to make, and Mexicans use them to turn anything into a taco.

1¾ cups *masa harina*

1⅛ cups hot water

1. In a medium bowl, mix together the *masa harina* and water until completely blended. Turn the dough onto a clean surface and knead until smooth. If the dough is too sticky, add more *masa harina*. If too dry, sprinkle with water. Cover the dough tightly with plastic wrap and let it stand for 30 minutes.

2. Preheat a cast-iron skillet or griddle to medium heat.

3. Divide the dough into walnut-sized balls. Using a tortilla press, a rolling pin, two heavy books, or your hands, press each ball of dough flat between two sheets of plastic wrap.

4. Place a tortilla in the preheated pan and cook for approximately 30 seconds, or until slightly browned. Turn the tortilla, cook the second side for about 30 seconds, and then transfer to a plate. Repeat the process with each ball of dough.

5. Keep the tortillas covered with a towel to stay warm and moist until you're ready to serve.

BASIC TORTILLA
Flour

YIELD: 12–16 TORTILLAS, DEPENDING ON SIZE

While corn tortillas are traditional in Mexico, flour tortillas are used in Baja California and along the U.S. border. When homemade, they can be delicious. The amount of water needed will vary with different types of flour. The dough should be firm and not sticky, like Play-Doh.

2 cups all-purpose flour

¼ cup vegetable shortening or lard, cut into pieces

½ teaspoon baking powder

½ teaspoon salt

¾ cup warm water

1. In a bowl, using two knives or a pastry blender, mix the flour, shortening, baking powder, and salt until it resembles fine meal. Add the water, a little at a time, and mix until the liquid is incorporated.

2. Form the dough into a ball and knead on a floured surface until the dough is smooth and elastic. Divide and make 12 smaller balls. Cover and let stand for at least 30 minutes.

3. Roll out each ball of dough on a floured surface to make 7-inch tortillas. Place on a preheated griddle or cast-iron skillet and cook until slightly golden on both sides and cooked through.

4. To make ahead: Remove the tortillas to a basket lined with a cloth towel, or put them between towels until cool. After the tortillas have cooled completely, store them in a plastic bag. Rewarm on a grill or griddle for a few seconds before serving.

BASIC TORTILLA
Cilantro

YIELD: 12-16 TORTILLAS, DEPENDING ON SIZE

Cilantro adds a special character to tortillas, but really, any herb can be used.
Basil is great, or you can try spinach.
Just remember to blot your greens very dry before using.

¼ cup cilantro leaves

1 recipe Basic Tortilla *Masa*

1. Blanch the cilantro in boiling water, shock it in cold water, squeeze dry, and mince. Prepare the *masa* according to the recipe (above), mix in the cilantro, roll the *masa* into 15 balls, and proceed according to the recipe.

2. Drain the beans and reserve the liquid. Using a potato masher or the back of a wooden spoon, mash the beans, along with some of the bean cooking liquid, until creamy but not completely mashed.

3. In a medium-size saucepan, heat the oil over medium-high heat. Sauté the onion with the oregano and a teaspoon of salt until golden brown, about 10 minutes. Add the mashed beans and cook, stirring occasionally, until the liquid evaporates and the beans form a mass that pulls away from the sides and bottom of the pan, about 10 minutes.

4. Transfer to the jar of an electric blender. With the motor running, purée the beans while adding the lemon olive oil in a steady stream. Season to taste with salt.

DOS CAMINOS'S HOUSE
Hot Sauce

YIELD: ABOUT 2 CUPS

Luscious, ripe mangoes shine in our very hot House Hot Sauce and, honestly, there's no other fruit that works as magically, especially when the fruit is ripe. If it's not totally mature, adjust the recipe with a little more sugar and a bit more salt. In a pinch, you could use a generous cup of defrosted frozen, unsweetened mangoes. Stored in a tightly covered container, it will keep in the refrigerator for a couple of days. If you prefer, use only two habañeros.

3 *habañero* chiles, coarsely chopped

1 *ripe* mango, peeled, pitted, and coarsely chopped

⅓ cup yellow mustard

1½ tablespoons firmly packed dark brown sugar

1½ tablespoons white vinegar

1 tablespoon ground *chiles de árbol*

1 teaspoon chile powder

1 teaspoon ground cumin

1 teaspoon yellow curry powder

1 teaspoon fine sea salt

Freshly ground black pepper

1. In the jar of an electric blender, combine the *habañeros,* mango, mustard, brown sugar, vinegar, *chiles de árbol,* chile powder, cumin, curry powder, and salt. Blend until smooth.

2. Scrape into a bowl, whisk in black pepper to taste, and adjust the salt level, if desired.

HOW TO PEEL AND CUT UP A MANGO

For starters, buy a mango with a little give to be sure it's ripe. Figure out which is the flat side of the mango: it corresponds with the wide side of the large seed inside. Stand the mango on one end and cut off the side as close to the seed as possible, making a large "cheek." Turn and cut off the other side along the seed. Pare away the remaining flesh around the edges in a crescent shape. Using a sharp paring knife, make crisscross cuts in the flesh, turn the skin inside out, and cut across the mango to make nice cubes. Or, once it's removed from the seed, you can scoop out the flesh with a large spoon and cut it into small cubes afterward.

SALSA VERDE

YIELD: 2 CUPS

Salsa Verde, or tomatillo salsa, is a fresh-tasting alternative to those made with tomatoes, and you might quickly become addicted to its citrusy taste. The fruit is a relative of tomatoes, but smaller, and grows inside a papery husk that must be removed before using. When totally cooled, this condiment may be refrigerated for up to 5 days or frozen in a well-sealed container for 6 months.

3 small tomatillos, husked, washed, and coarsely chopped

2 small cloves garlic, split

1 *jalapeño*, stemmed and coarsely chopped

1 medium white onion

2 tablespoons chopped cilantro

½ tablespoon freshly squeezed lime juice

Fine Sea Salt

1. In a medium saucepan, bring 2 quarts of water to a boil. Add the tomatillos, garlic, *jalapeño,* and onion. Simmer for 7 to 8 minutes, depending on size, and drain. Reserve the cooking liquid.

2. Transfer the tomatillos to the jar of an electric blender along with the cilantro, lime juice, and salt to taste, and puree until smooth, adding some of the cooking liquid, if needed, to achieve a smooth consistency. Return the mixture to the pan and simmer gently for 15 minutes. Taste to adjust the seasoning, as needed. Remove and serve cool.

ROASTED TOMATO
Chile de Árbol SALSA

YIELD: 4 CUPS

Probably the most commonly used chile for table salsa in Mexico, the ábol *chile is spicy and bright in flavor. It's also bright red, so it's used for a decorative element as well as good flavoring. This salsa is used several times in the book, and it's always delicious.*

4 ripe Roma tomatoes (about 1 pound)

2 unpeeled cloves garlic

1 medium white onion

1 *serrano* chile

1 *chile de árbol*, stemmed and seeded

1 teaspoon freshly squeezed lime juice

1 bunch fresh cilantro, coarse stems removed

Fine sea salt

1. Position a broiler rack 8 inches from the heat and preheat the broiler. Broil the tomatoes, garlic, onion, and *serrano* and *árbol* chiles until blackened all over. Leave the blackened skin on the vegetables.

2. Transfer the ingredients to the jar of an electric blender and pulse until coarsely chopped. Season to taste with salt.

Chipotle SALSA

YIELD: 4 CUPS

A chipotle *is a smoked* jalapeno. *This recipe uses canned* chipotles en adabo, *which are a great pantry staple. Dried, rehydrated chipotles would work as well here*

1 large white onion

¼ cup olive or blended oil or a mixture

4 cloves garlic

1 (28-ounce) can peeled tomatoes
    including juices

2 canned *chipotles en adobo*

1 bay leaf

1 teaspoon cumin seeds,
    toasted and ground

1 teaspoon dried *epazote,*
    or dried basil may be substituted

1 teaspoon dried oregano,
    preferably Mexican

1 teaspoon ground cinnamon,
    preferably Mexican *canela*

½ teaspoon freshly ground black pepper

⅛ teaspoon ground allspice

Fine sea salt to taste

1. Turn the broiler on. Lightly brush the onion with a little oil and broil it in a flat pan about 5 inches from the heat until soft and golden, turning once.

2. In a small skillet, heat a few drops of oil over medium heat. Add the garlic and sauté until soft and golden, shaking the pan occasionally.

3. Transfer the onion and garlic to the jar of an electric blender. Add the tomatoes, *chipotles,* bay leaf, cumin, *epazote,* oregano, cinnamon, pepper, and allspice; puree until smooth. Pour the mixture into a large saucepan and simmer for 30 minutes. Season to taste with salt.

TOMATILLO *Pasilla de Oaxaca* SALSA

YIELD: ABOUT 2 CUPS

This salsa is smoky-sweet and tart at the same time. Add a few teaspoons of mezcal for a really unique salsa. I put it on everything at home and it is especially nice served warm with chips on a cold day. It appears in several recipes throughout the book.

½ pound tomatillos, husked, rinsed, and quartered

1 teaspoon lard or blended oil

2 medium cloves garlic

3 small *pasilla de Oaxaca* chiles

Fine sea salt

2–3 teaspoons mezcal (optional)

1. In a small saucepan, combine the tomatillos with enough water to come about halfway up the sides of the tomatillos. Cover and cook over medium heat until the tomatillos are soft, about 10 minutes. Strain, reserving the liquid.

2. Meanwhile, on the *plancha* or in a heavy skillet, melt the lard or heat the oil and cook the garlic until soft and well charred on all sides, 5 to 10 minutes. Transfer to the jar of an electric blender.

3. Add the chiles to the *plancha* and toast for 2 minutes per side. Tear the chiles into pieces, discarding the stem and seeds, and transfer to the blender jar. Add the cooking liquid and a large pinch of salt to the jar and blend until smooth. Add the tomatillos, blend, and season with salt as necessary. Stir in mezcal, if using.

Pico de Gallo

YIELD: ABOUT 2 CUPS

Pico de Gallo, or Salsa Fresca, is the basic fresh uncooked tomato salsa that you'll use again and again. It's infinitely superior to any product packaged in a jar and takes minutes to make. Pico de Gallo translates to "Rooster's Beak." Nobody knowns the true origins of the name, but given the Mexican's love of nicknames, I like to think it comes from the chiles "pecking" at your tongue.

4 Roma tomatoes, cored, seeded, and finely diced

2 *jalapeños*, stemmed, seeded, and finely diced

1 red onion, finely diced

½ cup chopped cilantro leaves

2 tablespoons freshly squeezed lime juice

Fine sea salt

1. In a bowl, combine the tomatoes, *jalapeños*, onion, cilantro, and lime juice.

2. Season to taste with salt, cover, and refrigerate.

APPLE ONION
Pico de Gallo

YIELD: 2 CUPS

This citrus-scented blend of apples, onions, and jalapeños *is a refreshing complement to pork tacos. Honeycrisps are my favorite apples, but any variety of apples can be used."*

Juice of 1 lemon

2 Honeycrisp or Gala apples, peeled, cored, and julienned

1 Granny Smith apple, peeled, cored, and julienned

1 *jalapeño*, seeded and julienned

½ red onion, julienned

½ cup julienned cilantro

Juice of 1½ limes

Fine sea salt

1. Fill a bowl with cold water and add the lemon juice. Add the apples as you peel them to prevent them from turning brown.

2. Drain apples and blot dry. In a large bowl, combine the apples, *jalapeño*, onion, cilantro, lime juice, and salt to taste.

BLACK BEAN
Pico de Gallo

YIELD: 2½ CUPS

Once black beans (either just cooked or canned) are well rinsed to prevent the salsa from turning dark, you can appreciate the bright colors and flavors of tomatoes, corn, and onions accented with diced chorizo. The Spanish dried variety of the sausage is firmer than Mexican chorizo and has a mildly spicy taste. When refrigerated, the salsa lasts about 4 days.

1 ear corn, shucked

½ (8-ounce) link Spanish dried chorizo, preferably Palacios brand, split lengthwise

1 cup cooked black beans or canned black beans, well rinsed and drained

2 medium tomatoes, cored and diced

¼ cup chopped green onions, including most of the green parts

¼ cup diced red onion

¼ cup chopped cilantro

1 tablespoon minced *jalapeño* pepper

1 tablespoon freshly squeezed lime juice

1½ teaspoons *ancho* chile powder

1½ teaspoons extra-virgin olive oil

⅛ teaspoon fine sea salt

1. Grill the whole ear of corn on a grill or grill pan and cut from cob. You should have about ½ cup. Alternatively, using a sharp knife, cut the kernels from an ear of corn.

2. In a skillet, heat 1 teaspoon of oil over medium-high heat. Add the corn and cook until lightly charred, shaking the pan often. Remove and cool.

3. Wipe out the skillet, or use a grill, and heat. Add the chorizo and cook for 1 minute on each side, turning once. Remove, cool, and dice.

4. Place the beans, tomatoes, corn, green and red onions, cilantro, *jalapeño,* lime juice, chile powder, oil, and salt in a bowl. Add the cooled chorizo, and. stir to blend.

WATERMELON
Pico de Gallo

YIELD: 2½ CUPS

In the heat of late summer, when watermelons are at their best, switch up the tomatoes for this refreshing fruit. Salting the watermelon before adding the other ingredients will help to remove some of the moisture and keep the salsa from being watery. This is outstanding on grilled chicken or pork ribs.

dash fine sea salt

2 cups watermelon, cut into ½-inch cubes

2 *serrano* chiles, sliced paper-thin
   with seeds

2 tablespoons freshly squeezed lime juice

1½ tablespoons mint leaves,
   cut in chiffonade

1 teaspoon Maldon or other
   coarse sea salt

1. In a large bowl, sprinkle sea salt on the watermelon and turn to mix. Add the *serranos,* lime juice, mint leaves, and coarse salt.

2. Toss gently and refrigerate for 2 hours before using.

GUACAMOLE

YIELD: 2 CUPS

In Mexico, guacamole is more of a table condiment or salsa. Dos Caminos's guacamole is probably our most famous dish. It's been voted the best in many different polls. What makes ours so good? First, guacamole is at its best when made just before serving it. Another key to success is California-grown Hass avocados because they have a creamier, denser texture than all other varieties. This recipe may be multiplied as many times as you like. The spice level can be raised or lowered by adjusting the amount of chile you add. Generally figure that guacamole made with 1 avocado serves two; 2 serves four to six; 3 avocados serves six to eight.

2 tablespoons finely chopped cilantro leaves

2 teaspoons finely chopped white onion

2 teaspoons minced *jalapeño* or *serrano* chiles, seeds and membranes removed if desired

½ teaspoon kosher salt

2 large ripe avocados, preferably Hass variety, peeled and seeded

2 tablespoons cored, seeded, and finely chopped plum tomatoes (about 1 small tomato)

2 teaspoons freshly squeezed lime juice

1. In a medium-size bowl or *molcajete,* use the back of a spoon to mash 1 tablespoon of the cilantro, 1 teaspoon onion, 1 teaspoon of minced chile, and ½ teaspoon salt together against the bottom of the bowl.

2. Add the avocados and gently mash them with a fork until chunky-smooth.

3. Fold the remaining cilantro, onion, and chile into the mixture.

4. Stir in the tomatoes and lime juice, taste to adjust the seasonings, and serve with a basket of warm corn tortilla chips or *chicharonnes* (see page 156).

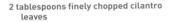

DOS CAMINOS *Tacos*

44

AVOCADO
Aioli

YIELD: 1½ CUPS

When you blend creamy avocados mixed with mayonnaise and serrano chile with lime juice,
you get this zesty aioli that can be used on all kinds of tacos. I love it on fish and poultry.
It may be prepared up to 8 hours ahead of time and refrigerated in an
airtight container to prevent oxidation. The heat level of serrano (and other) chiles
can vary between hot and milder temperatures. Depending on the time of year,
and the amount of chiles used in a recipe, you may want to start by adding a little less
to a recipe and then increasing the amount after you verify the intensity.

1 large, ripe avocado, preferably Hass variety, peeled and pitted

½ cup mayonnaise, not light variety

½ *serrano* chile

Zest and juice of 1 large lime

Fine sea salt

1. In the jar of an electric blender, puree the avocado, mayonnaise, chile, and zest and juice of the lime until smooth.

2. Scrape into a bowl, season to taste with salt, and serve.

Chipotle AÍOLI

YIELD: 2 CUPS

*We use this as a final drizzle on many tacos.
It is particularly good with seafood. It also makes a fantastic sandwich spread.
Try it on a cheeseburger — yum!*

2 cups mayonnaise, not light variety

4 canned *chipotles en adobo*

4 cloves garlic, chopped

¼ cup chopped fresh dill

¼ cup freshly squeezed lime juice

Fine sea salt

1. In the jar of an electric blender, combine the mayonnaise, *chipotles en adobo*, garlic, dill, and lime juice.

2. Puree until smooth and season to taste with salt.

Cracked BLACK PEPPER
Aioli

YIELD: 2 CUPS

*The tiny bits of peppercorns and thyme leaves in this creamy aioli
(it never becomes totally smooth) make this sauce an exciting accent for fish tacos
and oven-roasted fish fillets. If you're using store-bought, use commercial mayonnaise,
not salad dressings or spreads, which are too thin.*

½ cup freshly cracked black peppercorns

3 tablespoons sherry wine vinegar

2 tablespoons finely chopped
    fresh thyme leaves

3 cloves garlic, minced

1½ cups mayonnaise, not light variety

Fine sea salt

Cayenne pepper

1. In a food processor, puree the pepper, vinegar, thyme, and garlic until almost smooth. Scrape into a small bowl.

2. Whisk in the mayonnaise, season with salt and a touch of cayenne pepper, cover, and refrigerate until needed.

BACON-FAT-PICKLED
Jalapeño MAYONNAISE

YIELD: 2½ CUPS

*Bacon makes everything taste good. Once the tasty strips are cooked,
reserve the rendered fat for later use, such as this mayonnaise with a tangy hit of pickled jalapeños.
Strain bacon fat and store it in the refrigerator, then let it return to room temperature, a liquid state,
before using. This mayonnaise keeps for at least a month in the refrigerator but it will
probably be used up long before that.*

5 large egg yolks

1 tablespoon Dijon mustard

7 teaspoons freshly squeezed lemon juice, divided

1½ cups rendered bacon fat, at room temperature

3 tablespoons finely diced pickled *jalapeños*

½ teaspoon fine sea salt

Freshly ground black pepper

1. Chill all of the ingredients and utensils down to about 40 degrees. Don't skip this step or the mayonnaise may break.

2. In the jar of an electric blender, combine the egg yolks, mustard, and 1½ teaspoons of the lemon juice. Blend on high until totally mixed, about 2 minutes.

3. Add the bacon fat in a slow stream, continuing to blend until the mixture is thick. Blend in the remaining lemon juice, *jalapeños*, salt, and pepper to taste. Adjust the seasonings according to taste. Scrape into a bowl, cover, and refrigerate until needed.

ANCHO CHILE
Vinaigrette

YIELD: 2 CUPS

Use this lively vinaigrette to pop up the taste of lettuce on top of a taco or as a dressing for a salad with oranges, avocados, and watercress. When cooled and stored in a covered glass jar, the dressing will keep in your refrigerator for 10 days to 2 weeks. Substitute chipotle chiles for a smoky vinaigrette for a spinach salad.

1 cup blended oil

¾ cup rice vinegar

½ cup honey

¼ cup Dijon mustard

1 tablespoon rehydrated and pureed *ancho* chile

1 tablespoon toasted sesame oil

3 tablespoons chopped fresh cilantro

2 tablespoons freshly squeezed lime juice

1½ tablespoons minced red bell pepper

1 tablespoon minced red onion

¼ teaspoon freshly ground black pepper

Fine sea salt to taste

1. In a glass bowl, stir the oil, vinegar, honey, mustard, *ancho* chile puree, sesame oil, cilantro, lime juice, red bell pepper, onion, black pepper, and salt to taste until blended.

2. Heat the dressing in the microwave on high until the mixture begins to bubble, 1 to 1½ minutes.

3. Remove and whisk for 1 minute to emulsify the dressing. It should thicken as it cools.

4. Cover and chill for 2 hours before serving.

Cilantro CREMA

YIELD: 2½ CUPS

Cilantro crema *is a lively, flavorful addition to dishes when plain sour cream would be mundane.*
Crema *is Mexican sour cream. If you can't find it, I think American sour cream thinned with*
heavy cream to a smoother consistency is a good solution. Greek yogurt is the best substitute
but you can also use crème fraîche in most recipes. It'll keep in the refrigerator for 3 days.

3 tablespoons chopped fresh cilantro

1 tablespoon minced scallions,
including green parts

1 teaspoon seeded and minced
serrano chile

2 cups *crema* or sour cream thinned
with a little cream

1 teaspoon fine sea salt

1. In the jar of an electric blender, combine the cilantro, scallions, and *serrano* chile; puree until smooth.

2. Scrape into a bowl, fold in the *crema* and salt, cover, and refrigerate until needed.

CHEF'S TIPS:

If you save trimmings and leftovers, use epazote *stems in a stock*
or sauce to impart a nice herbaceous flavor.

Epazote CREMA

YIELD: 2 CUPS

Epazote *is commonly used in Mexican cooking, especially in bean dishes, as well as in mole and soups. It also makes a good tea for an upset stomach. Its flavor is similar to that of oregano. If you can't find it fresh, substitute about half the amount of the dried herb. If you place it in a covered bowl, this sauce will keep for up to a week in the refrigerator.*

½ pound *epazote,* stems removed

1½ cups sour cream

¼ cup milk

1 teaspoon kosher salt

1. In a large bowl, combine the *epazote* with just enough boiling water to cover. Mix well and let sit for 1 minute.

2. Drain and shock the *epazote* in ice water to set the color. Blot dry and transfer to the jar of an electric blender along with the sour cream, milk, and salt. Blend until smooth. The *crema* should be bright green. Scrape into a bowl, cover, and refrigerate until needed.

APPLE-CRANBERRY
Salsita

YIELD: ABOUT 3½ CUPS

The fruity sweet and tangy flavors of this delectable salsita *make it a perfect condiment for rich meats such as duck or pork belly (page 212).* Piloncillo *is unrefined Mexican dark brown sugar sold in solid cones with flattened tops that resemble the tower-like pylons used to anchor above-ground power lines. Sizes range from under an ounce to more than half a pound. One six-ounce cone measures about 1 cup. While firmer in texture than American brown sugar, the two can be used interchangeably, but* piloncillo *should be chopped with a serrated knife before using.*

5 Granny Smith apples, peeled, cored, and diced

2 cups apple cider vinegar

1 cup chopped *piloncillo* or firmly packed dark brown sugar

1 cup dried cranberries

2 *serrano* chiles, sliced paper thin on a mandolin

¼ cup diced red onion

1 tablespoon chopped cilantro

Juice of 1 lime

Fine sea salt

1. In a non-reactive pan, combine the apples, vinegar, and *piloncillo* and simmer over medium heat until the apples begin to soften, 2 to 3 minutes. Remove with a slotted spoon to a bowl to cool.

2. Add the dried cranberries to the liquid and simmer until they are rehydrated and begin to soften. Transfer from the liquid to the bowl with the apples and set aside to cool.

3. Over high heat, reduce the remaining liquid by half and set aside to cool.

4. Gently combine the *serrano* chiles, onion, and cilantro with the apples and cranberries. Toss in the cooled liquid with the lime juice and season to taste with salt.

GRILLED PEACH *and* RED PEPPER *Salsita*

YIELD: ABOUT 2½ CUPS

This chunky, rustic salsita *is a boon for pork, grilled skirt steak, and brisket tacos. Refrigerated, it will keep for at least 4 days.*

¼ cup extra-virgin olive oil

½ bunch finely chopped fresh basil (about ½ cup)

2 tablespoons finely chopped fresh mint

2 cloves garlic, minced

Salt and freshly ground black pepper

1 pound firm but ripe peaches, halved and pitted

2 large red bell peppers, quartered, seeds and membranes removed

1 *habañero* pepper, seeded

1 tablespoon apple cider vinegar

1. Light a barbecue or position a broiler rack 8 inches from the heat and preheat the the broiler.

2. In a small bowl, combine the oil, basil, mint, and garlic. Season to taste with salt and pepper. Lightly brush the cut side of the peaches with half of the oil mixture. Grill or broil the peaches, cut side only, until lightly browned, watching closely to avoid burning, 2 minutes. Remove with tongs to a bowl and let cool.

3. Grill or broil the skin side of the peppers until charred and blistered, about 8 minutes. Using tongs, remove to a bowl and cover with a cloth. When cool, pull off the skin.

4. Cut the peaches and peppers into ½-inch pieces. Transfer to medium bowl, add the vinegar and remaining oil mixture, season to taste with salt and pepper, and toss gently to blend.

VEGETARIAN

Tacos

GRILLED ASPARAGUS *and* AVOCADO TACOS

YIELD: 12 TACOS

After a chilly spring in New York, as a chef I was dreaming of the great produce of the season that had been slow to arrive. When I finally came across some beautiful purple-tipped asparagus at the Union Square Greenmarket, I almost cried. I really wanted to make a taco with them. In Mexico asparagus is common in the markets, and everything eventually becomes a taco! Rich, creamy California Hass avocados also make their debut in spring and are a perfect complement to asparagus.

Although the result was not a traditional taco, it represents how I was feeling— the Mediterranean flavors were inspired by a longing for the warmth of the sun and the coming summer. Gently grilling asparagus and avocado adds a light smoky flavor to them and gets you out of doors.

Refried White Beans *(recipe follows)*

Cucumber *Pico de Gallo (recipe follows)*

12 large asparagus spears,
   woody ends removed

1–2 tablespoons olive oil

Fine sea salt

2 ripe avocados, preferably Hass variety

12 corn tortillas, preferably handmade,
   warmed on the grill

¼ cup crumbled *queso fresco*

1. Prepare the Refried White Beans and Cucumber *Pico de Gallo*. Light a grill or heat a grill pan until hot.

2. Drizzle the asparagus with oil and sprinkle with salt, turning to coat evenly. Lay the asparagus on the grill and cook until small brown spots form on the spears, turning several times to cook them evenly, 5 to 6 minutes total cooking time. Remove, cut them in half, and tent to keep warm.

3. If space allows, prepare the avocados alongside the asparagus. Using a sharp knife, cut the avocados in half lengthwise. To remove the pit, cut deeply enough into it so you can turn the knife; the pit will come loose. Peel the avocado halves, brush with a little oil, and grill them, flesh-side down, until grill marks appear on the avocados and they are warm, 2 to 5 minutes. Remove and cut each into six slices.

4. Spoon about 2 tablespoons of Refried White Beans into each tortilla. Lay an asparagus spear on the white beans, add an avocado slice, and garnish with about a teaspoon each of the Cucumber *Pico de Gallo* and *queso fresco*. Pass extra beans and *Pico de Gallo* at the table.

REFRIED WHITE BEANS

1 cup dried cannellini beans,
  rinsed and stones, dirt,
  and shriveled beans discarded

2 *serrano* chiles, split

1 tablespoon olive oil

1 medium white onion, diced

½ teaspoon dried oregano,
  preferably Mexican

Fine sea salt

2 teaspoons lemon olive oil
  (see the sidebar)

CUCUMBER *PICO DE GALLO*

2 Kirby cucumbers, ends trimmed,
  peeled, and finely diced

2 Roma tomatoes, cored and finely diced

1 small red onion, finely diced

1 *jalapeño* pepper, finely chopped

1 *serrano* chile, finely chopped

¼ cup freshly squeezed lime juice

2 teaspoons extra-virgin olive oil

1 teaspoon lemon olive oil
  (see the sidebar)

Fine sea salt

Refried White Beans

1. In a medium-sized pot, bring 4 cups of water to a boil. Add the beans and *serranos,* reduce the water to a simmer, cover, and cook until the beans are cooked through and creamy inside, approximately 1 hour and 45 minutes, skimming the foam from the top occasionally. To test for doneness, taste three or four of the smaller beans.

2. Drain the beans and reserve the liquid. Remove the chiles if desired. Using a potato masher or the back of a wooden spoon, mash the beans, along with some of the bean cooking liquid, until creamy but not completely mashed.

3. In a medium-sized saucepan, heat the oil over medium-high heat. Sauté the onion with the oregano and 1 teaspoon of salt until golden brown, about 10 minutes. Add the mashed beans and cook, stirring occasionally, until the liquid evaporates and the beans form a mass that pulls away from the sides and bottom of the pan, about 10 minutes.

4. Transfer to the jar of an electric blender. With the motor running, puree the beans while adding the lemon olive oil in a steady stream. Season to taste with salt.

Cucumber *Pico de Gallo*

Combine the cucumbers, tomatoes, onion, *jalapeño,* and *serrano* with the lime juice, oil, lemon oil, and salt to taste. Let stand for 30 minutes before serving.

LEMON OLIVE OIL

While you can buy bottles of lemon-scented olive oil, it's easy enough to make your own. Wash and thoroughly dry a large lemon. Remove only the brightly colored yellow part of the skin and combine it with a cup of olive oil in a small saucepan. Warm over medium heat, not even letting it simmer, for about 10 minutes. Remove and cool, then strain the oil into a clean jar. Cover and store in a cool dark place.

AVOCADO *Tacos* BAJA-STYLE *with* CITRUS-CUCUMBER *Slaw*

YIELD: 16 TACOS

I often sing the praises of avocados—especially the buttery Hass variety. While frequently second fiddle and/or used as a garnish, except in guacamole, here they star in these tempura-coated slices. Besides being delicious, avocados are rich in nutrients and healthful fats. To keep them from turning brown: Don't cut the fruit until you're ready to use it.

Citrus-Cucumber Slaw *(recipe follows)*

1 cup all-purpose flour, plus flour
   for dredging the avocado slices

1 cup cornstarch

2 teaspoons baking powder

2 teaspoons baking soda

2 teaspoons sugar

1 teaspoon fine sea salt

2 large eggs

Blended oil for frying

4 ripe avocados, preferably Hass variety,
   peeled and pitted

16 flour tortillas, warmed

Valentina or other hot sauce

4 limes, quartered, for garnish

1. In a medium-sized bowl, whisk the flour, cornstarch, baking powder, baking soda, sugar, and salt together. In a separate mixing bowl, whisk the eggs and 1 ⅓ cups of cold water together. Beat the dry ingredients into the eggs. The batter will be a little lumpy.

2. Fill a large skillet with enough oil for deep-frying. You should be able to submerge the avocado slices completely in oil in the pan. Heat the oil to 375 degrees on an instant-read thermometer. Halve the avocados and slice each half lengthwise into four slices.

3. Lightly coat the avocado slices in a little flour and then dip them into the tempura batter, letting the excess fall off. Using tongs, carefully place the avocado slices into the hot oil and fry until golden. Remove, drain on paper towels, and salt to taste.

4. Fill the tortillas and serve garnished with Citrus-Cucumber Slaw and plenty of hot sauce and limes on the side.

CHEF'S TIPS:

If you don't have a thermometer to gauge the oil's temperature for deep-fat frying, you can test when it's ready by dropping a 1-inch cube of white bread into the pan. At the right temperature, the oil should brown the bread in 60 seconds.

CITRUS-CUCUMBER SLAW

3 Kirby cucumbers, peeled, seeded, and cut into thin strips

3 Roma tomatoes, cored, seeded, and cut into thin strips

1 small red onion, cut into thin strips

1 *serrano* chile, thinly sliced

1 cup finely shredded white cabbage

¼ cup chopped cilantro leaves

½ cup freshly squeezed orange juice

2 tablespoons freshly squeezed grapefruit juice

1 tablespoon freshly squeezed lime juice

1 tablespoon fine sea salt

Citrus-Cucumber Slaw

In a non-reactive bowl, combine the cucumbers, tomatoes, onion, chile, cabbage, and cilantro. Blend the orange, grapefruit, and lime juices together and pour over the vegetables. Add the salt, toss to blend well, and set aside for 30 minutes.

BLUE CHEESE, WALNUT, and CABBAGE Tacos

YIELD: 10 TACOS

This autumnal or winter taco makes great party fare. The robust Gorgonzola and walnuts perfectly complement sweet and tangy sautéed cabbage. Serve with ice-cold dry sherry or one of the great boutique wines from the Valle de Guadalupe, Mexico's wine-making region.

½ head red cabbage, cored and julienned

½ white onion, minced

1 *jalapeño*, seeded and minced

1 cup apple cider vinegar

½ cup sugar

1 tablespoon whole-grain mustard

½ tablespoon fine sea salt

1 teaspoon prepared horseradish

1 teaspoon ground cinnamon, preferably Mexican *canela*

1 teaspoon ground allspice

⅓ cup crumbled Gorgonzola cheese

¼ cup chopped walnuts, toasted

10 corn tortillas, warmed

1. In a large saucepan, combine the cabbage, onion, *jalapeño,* vinegar, sugar, mustard, salt, horseradish, *canela,* allspice, and ½ cup of water. Bring to a boil, reduce the heat to a simmer, cover, and cook until the cabbage is tender, about 1 hour. Remove the pan from the heat, let the cabbage cool, and drain.

2. In a mixing bowl, combine the cabbage with the Gorgonzola and walnuts and set aside. Spoon the mixture into the tortillas and serve.

BUTTERNUT SQUASH
Cotija Tacos

YIELD: 12 TACOS

Roasted butternut squash and Cotija *cheese are a delicious and savory combination, especially when accented with fresh rosemary. I love them with* Grilled Nopales *Salad (page 230) on the side.*

2 tablespoons olive oil

1 butternut squash, about 2 pounds, cut in half lengthwise and seeded

2 sprigs rosemary

1 large shallot, minced

3 cloves garlic, minced

1 cup crumbled *Cotija* cheese

12 corn tortillas, warmed

Fine sea salt and freshly ground black pepper

1. The night before, prepare the Grilled *Nopales* Salad, if using.

2. Heat the oven to 350 degrees.

3. Lightly brush a jelly-roll pan and the insides of the squash halves with 1 tablespoon of the oil. Put a rosemary sprig in each cavity, lay the squash skin-side down in the pan, and roast until tender when poked with a fork or knife, 30 minutes or up to 1 hour. Remove from the oven, scoop out the flesh, and mash until chunky-smooth.

4. In a large skillet, heat the remaining oil over medium-high heat. Add the shallot and garlic and cook for 2 minutes. Stir in the squash and cheese; season to taste with salt and pepper. Spoon into the tortillas and serve.

VARIATIONS: Use 1 cup roasted or leftover cooked pumpkin or yams. If desired, add black beans and *epazote,* or cilantro, sautéed onions, and roasted bell peppers.

COLLARD GREENS *Tacos* with PICKLED APPLES *and* WALNUTS

YIELD: 12 TACOS

When days are cool, these hearty tacos of collard greens accented with pickled apples and walnuts make a warming Sunday supper. Swiss chard or kale make fine substitutions if you don't find collard greens. Close your eyes and be transported to the warmth of Mexico.

2 red apples, such as Gala

½ cup apple cider vinegar

½ cup sugar

2 *jalapeños*, split

1 teaspoon fine sea salt

1 teaspoon pickling spice

½ cup walnut halves

¼ cup olive oil

1 pound collard greens

½ teaspoon kosher salt

Freshly ground black pepper

12 corn tortillas, warmed

1. Core and quarter the apples, then cut each quarter lengthwise into ⅛-inch-thick slices. In a non-reactive saucepan, stir the vinegar and sugar together with 1 cup of water. Add the *jalapeños,* salt, and pickling spice; boil until the sugar is dissolved. Stir in the apples and return to a boil. Transfer to a heatproof bowl and cool. Chill, uncovered, until cold, about 1 hour.

2. While the apples chill, prepare the nuts: In a small skillet over medium heat, toast the walnuts in the oil until they're one shade darker, stirring occasionally. Remove from the heat and cool in the oil. Using a slotted spoon, transfer the nuts to a cutting board, reserving the oil. Coarsely chop 1 tablespoon of the nuts and finely chop the remaining nuts. Set aside. Reserve the oil.

3. With kitchen shears or a sharp knife, halve each collard leaf lengthwise, cutting out and discarding the center ribs. Stack the leaves and cut them crosswise into ¼-inch-wide strips. Transfer to a large bowl.

4. In a deep skillet, heat the oil from the walnuts over medium-high heat until hot. Add the collard greens and sauté until slightly cooked but not wilted, 3 to 4 minutes. Stir in the nuts and toss with ½ teaspoon of salt and pepper to taste. Add the apple slices, discarding the pickling liquid and spices, and toss again. Spoon into the tortillas and serve.

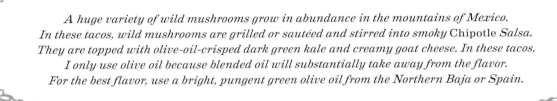

Grilled WILD MUSHROOM and KALE Tacos

YIELD: 8 TACOS

*A huge variety of wild mushrooms grow in abundance in the mountains of Mexico.
In these tacos, wild mushrooms are grilled or sautéed and stirred into smoky* Chipotle *Salsa.
They are topped with olive-oil-crisped dark green kale and creamy goat cheese. In these tacos,
I only use olive oil because blended oil will substantially take away from the flavor.
For the best flavor, use a bright, pungent green olive oil from the Northern Baja or Spain.*

1 cup *Chipotle* Salsa (page 35)

2¼ pounds mixed wild mushrooms,
    cleaned and trimmed

2 tablespoons olive oil,
    plus 3 tablespoons for the kale

Fine sea salt and freshly ground
    black pepper

1 small bunch kale (about 8 ounces),
    stemmed and cut into chiffonade

8 corn tortillas, warmed

½ cup crumbled goat cheese,
    seasoned with black pepper

1. Prepare the *Chipotle* Salsa and keep warm.

2. Heat a gas grill or large heavy skillet over medium-high heat. In a large bowl, toss the mushrooms in the 2 tablespoons of oil, and grill or sauté them in the skillet until just cooked through and browned. Remove, cut into slices, season with salt and pepper, and spoon *Chipotle* Salsa to taste on top of them.

3. In a large skillet, heat the remaining oil until hot. Add the kale and cook until crisp, turning often. Season to taste with salt and pepper.

4. Spoon the mushrooms onto the tortillas, garnish with the kale and goat cheese, and serve.

Huitlacoche and MUSHROOM Tacos

YIELD: 12 TACOS

In Mexico, the rare corn fungus known as huitlacoche *is as highly prized as truffles are in Europe. The kernels have a smoky-sweet flavor and are best when bought fresh or frozen. I serve the tacos with* Salsa Verde Cruda, *probably Mexico's most popular sauce. Any extra salsa can be eaten with tortilla chips or kept in the refrigerator for a day.*

Salsa Verde Cruda (recipe follows)

2 teaspoons blended oil, divided

1 cup minced white onions

1 tablespoon chopped garlic

1 cup *huitlacoche*, coarsely chopped

1 teaspoon ground *chile de árbol*

2½ cups sliced mushrooms, such as shiitake, cremini, or any flavorful mushrooms

¼ cup chopped fresh *epazote* or cilantro

Fine sea salt

12 corn tortillas, warmed

6 ounces *queso Oaxaca*, Mexican string cheese, pulled into fine strings

Crema, Greek yogurt, or crème fraîche, for garnish

SALSA VERDE CRUDA

1¼ pounds tomatillos, husked, washed, and coarsely chopped

4 cloves garlic

1 *serrano* chile, seeded, if desired

1 *jalapeño* chile, seeded, if desired

1 small white onion, coarsely chopped

¼ cup chopped cilantro

Fine sea salt

1. Make the *Salsa Verde Cruda.*

2. In a medium-sized skillet over high heat, add 1 teaspoon of oil and the minced onions; sauté until translucent, about 3 minutes. Stir in the garlic and continue to cook until it starts to brown, then add the *huitlacoche* and chile and simmer until all of the liquid has evaporated, about 5 minutes.

3. In a separate skillet over high heat, add the remaining oil and mushrooms and sauté until nicely browned. Stir in the *epazote,* cook for 1 minute, and season to taste with salt. Combine the mushrooms and onions in one skillet and stir to blend.

4. Spoon the mixture into the tortillas, top with *queso Oaxaca,* spoon on some *Salsa Verde Cruda,* drizzle with a little *crema,* and serve.

Salsa Verde Cruda
YIELD: ABOUT 3 CUPS

In a food processor, combine the tomatillos, garlic, *serrano* and *jalapeño* chiles, onion, and cilantro; pulse until chunky-smooth. Pour the salsa through a fine strainer, straining out most of the excess liquid. Transfer to a container, season to taste with salt, and refrigerate for up to 1 day.

WILD MUSHROOM and Nopales FILLED Tacos

YIELD: 12 TACOS

Creamy wild mushrooms (in whatever combination you like) blended with grilled cactus paddles, or nopales, *create a robust taco filling that's both earthy and indulgent. This filling is also great for an omelet. Be careful when cleaning the* Nopales, *they can be quite prickly.*

½ pound shiitake mushrooms, stemmed and wiped

½ pound cremini mushrooms, stemmed and wiped

½ pound oyster mushrooms, trimmed and wiped

¾ cup chopped white onion

¼ cup finely chopped *jalapeños*

2½ tablespoons finely chopped garlic

Fine sea salt

¾ cup blended oil or olive oil

2 ounces silver tequila, preferably Patrón, but not the cheap stuff

1 cup sour cream

½ cup heavy cream

2½ tablespoons cornstarch

½ pound *nopales*, grilled and finely diced

12 corn tortillas, warmed

Sliced cilantro leaves and *chile de árbol* powder, for garnish

1. Chop the mushrooms in two or four pieces depending on their size. Combine the mushrooms, onion, *jalapeños,* garlic, and 1 to 2 teaspoons of salt.

2. In a very large, heavy skillet, heat the oil over high heat. Add the mushrooms and sauté until all of the liquid has evaporated and they are richly browned and crispy looking, 12 to 15 minutes, shaking the pan often.

3. Pour in the tequila, carefully ignite, and cook until the liquid evaporates. Stir in the sour cream.

4. In a saucepan, bring the heavy cream to a simmer, whisk in the cornstarch, and return to a boil. Strain the cream over the mushrooms and simmer for about 20 minutes. Stir in the *nopales,* remove from the heat, and spoon into the tortillas. Garnish with a little cilantro and *chile de árbol* powder and serve.

SWEET POTATO *and* COLORADO
Bean Hash Tacos

YIELD: 16 TACOS

This hearty blend of sweet potatoes, peppers, and kidney beans will satisfy even the strongest appetites. It's a great dish for dark winter days along with a tossed green salad. Growing up, I knew red kidney beans as Colorado beans, probably because the word colorado *means "reddish" in Spanish. Colorado is known for its red sandstone landscape, and perhaps that's where the name comes from.*

2 tablespoons blended oil or olive oil or a combination of both

1 white onion, cut into medium dice

3 cloves garlic, thinly sliced

1 red bell pepper, seeded and cut into medium dice

1 *poblano* chile, seeded and cut into medium dice

2 *serrano* chiles, thinly sliced

1 teaspoon ground cinnamon

1 teaspoon ground coriander

1 teaspoon ground cumin

1 (8-ounce) undrained can red kidney beans

2 large sweet potatoes or yams, peeled and cut into large dice

2 Roma tomatoes, cored, seeded, and cut into medium dice

Fine sea salt

16 corn tortillas, warmed

1 cup crumbled *queso Menonita*

1. In a medium saucepan, heat the oil over high heat. Add the onion and sauté until it begins to caramelize. Stir in the garlic, bell and chile peppers, cinnamon, coriander, and cumin; sauté until the peppers are soft.

2. Add the beans and 1 cup of water. Bring the mixture to a simmer, add the sweet potatoes and tomatoes, season with salt, and simmer until the potatoes are fork-tender and the mixture is the consistency of a thick stew.

3. Spoon the mixture into the tortillas, drizzle on a little *queso Menonita,* and serve.

ROASTED PEPPER *and* CHILE *Tacos* POTOSINAS-STYLE *with* TOMATILLO *Pasilla de Oaxaca* SALSA

YIELD: 12 TACOS

The filling for these tacos was adapted from the beloved empanadas sold in the markets in the beautiful city of St. Luis Potosí in north-central Mexico. It's a colorful marriage of roasted sweet bell peppers and chiles along with a couple of creamy and tangy cheeses.

Basic Tortilla Cilantro (page 26)

Tomatillo *Pasilla de Oaxaca* Salsa (page 36)

2 tablespoons blended oil

2 cloves garlic, minced

1 small white onion, finely chopped

2 *poblano* chiles, roasted, peeled, seeded, and julienned

1 *jalapeño*, seeded and minced

1 red bell pepper, roasted, peeled, seeds and membranes removed, and cut into strips

1 yellow bell pepper, roasted, peeled, seeds and membranes removed, and cut into strips

4 ounces *requesón* or ricotta cheese

1 ounce *queso Chihuahua* or Monterey Jack cheese, grated

1 unpeeled red potato (about 3 ounces), cut into ¼-inch cubes and fried until golden

2 tablespoons julienned fresh *epazote*, plus 1 tablespoon for garnish

2 *costeño* chiles, toasted and crumbled

Fine sea salt

½ cup crumbled *Cotija* cheese, for garnish (optional)

½ cup *crema*, for garnish (optional)

1. Prepare the Basic Tortilla Cilantro.

2. Prepare the Tomatillo *Pasilla de Oaxaca Salsa.*

3. In a large skillet over medium-high heat, heat the oil until hot. Add the garlic and onion and sauté until the onion begins to color. Add the *poblanos, jalapeño,* and red and yellow peppers, and sauté until limp. Cool to room temperature. Transfer to a large bowl, stir in the *requesón* and Chihuahua cheeses, the potato, 2 tablespoons *epazote*, and the *costeño* chiles. Season to taste with salt.

4. Divide the filling among the tortillas. Spoon on some Tomatillo *Pasilla de Oaxaca* Salsa, sprinkle with *Cotija* cheese, and a little bit of the remaining *epazote*, and drizzle on a little *crema* before serving.

VEGETARIAN *Tacos*

PLANTAIN GOAT CHEESE *Gorditas with* ROASTED TOMATO *Chile de Árbol* SALSA

YIELD: 12 GORDITAS

Vegetarians and meat lovers alike will savor these "fat little tacos," or gorditas, *with sweet, salty, and spicy tastes encased in disks of plantain "dough." The masa cakes, like a tortilla, can be stuffed with just about anything you like.*

Roasted Tomato *Chile de Árbol* Salsa (page 34)

4 very ripe (almost black) soft plantains (about 2¼ pounds total), rinsed

2 tablespoons dry bread crumbs

1 teaspoon fine sea salt

¼ cup crumbled goat cheese

Blended oil for frying

Habañero Pickled Red Onions *(recipe follows)*

Crema, Greek yogurt, or crème fraîche, for garnish

HABAÑERO PICKLED RED ONIONS

2 large red onions, thinly sliced

1 small beet, peeled and quartered

1 *habañero* chile, cut in half

1 cup apple cider vinegar

2 bay leaves

1 teaspoon kosher salt

1. Prepare the Roasted Tomato *Chile de Árbol* Salsa.

2. Bring a large pot of water to a boil. Add the plantains and cook over medium-high heat until the skins split and the plantains are very tender when pierced with a knife, about 15 minutes. Transfer to a plate and let them cool slightly. Peel, transfer to a bowl, and mash well. Stir in the bread crumbs and salt and let cool.

3. Line a platter with plastic wrap. Form the plantain dough into 12 portions and roll into balls slightly smaller than a golf ball. Poke a hole in the center of each ball and fill it with 1 teaspoon of the goat cheese. Seal the holes and reroll the dough into balls. Using your hands, press the balls into round disks about 3 inches in diameter. Set the *gorditas* on the platter.

4. In a large saucepan, heat the oil to 350 degrees. Add the *gorditas* one after the other and fry until browned all over, about 5 minutes. Drain on a paper-towel-lined plate. Serve the *gorditas* with the Roasted Tomato *Chile de Árbol* Salsa, *Habañero* Pickled Red Onions, and *crema*.

Habañero Pickled Red Onions

YIELD: 3 CUPS

In a medium-sized non-reactive pan, combine the onions, beet, chile, vinegar, bay leaves, salt, and 1 cup of water; bring to a boil over medium heat. Remove from the heat and refrigerate for at least 1 hour or preferably overnight prior to using.

CANELA APPLESAUCE

3 pounds Golden Delicious apples, peeled, cored, and cut into ¾-inch pieces

⅓ cup firmly packed light brown sugar

2½ tablespoons freshly squeezed lemon juice

1 teaspoon vanilla extract

½ teaspoon ground cinnamon, preferably Mexican *canela*

Pinch of fine sea salt

Canela Applesauce

1. In a heavy medium-sized saucepan, combine the apples and brown sugar with 1 cup of water and bring to boil, stirring occasionally. Reduce the heat, cover, and simmer until the apples are very tender, about 25 minutes. Uncover and simmer until almost all the liquid has evaporated, about 6 minutes.

2. Remove the pan from the heat and stir in the lemon juice, vanilla, and cinnamon. Add the salt and cool for 30 minutes. Using a fork, mash the apple mixture until it is coarse and chunky.

VEGETARIAN *Tacos*

PURSLANE *Tacos*

YIELD: 12 TACOS

I really like purslane. Its slightly crunchy, somewhat lemony-tasting leaves,
also known as verdolagas, *are frequently found at farmers' markets in Mexico.*
(It's also common in backyards in the United States, where it's often thought of as a weed.)
High in vitamin E, these leaves are similar to watercress or spinach and are used interchangeably.
Besides being sautéed or steamed to fill these tacos or as a side dish, young purslane
can be stewed with meat or poultry, or used in salads and to top sandwiches.

1 pound fresh purslane

1 tablespoon blended oil

1 small white onion, finely chopped

1 teaspoon finely chopped fresh garlic

2–3 medium Roma tomatoes,
   depending on size, cored and chopped

1 *serrano* chile, finely chopped

2–3 tablespoons Maggi sauce

12 corn tortillas, warmed

1. Set aside a few raw sprigs of purslane for garnish. Steam or blanch the rest until crisp-tender, 3 to 5 minutes. Drain thoroughly, transfer to a plate covered with several layers of paper towels, and blot dry.

2. In a large pan, heat the oil over medium-high heat. Add the onion and garlic and sauté until soft. Stir in the tomatoes and chile and sauté until the mixture resembles a sauce. Season with Maggi and continue to cook until the mixture is warm and the flavors blend. Spoon into the tortillas and serve the tacos garnished with the remaining sprigs of purslane.

SPINACH á la GALLEGA Tacos

YIELD: 8 TACOS

Galician-style spinach traditionally made with currants and pine nuts is among our most popular side dishes and seemed a natural for vegetarian tacos. Here I added crumbled goat cheese and Tomatillo Pasilla de Oaxaca Salsa to the tasty mixture. For brunch, you might serve these alongside scrambled eggs.

Tomatillo *Pasilla de Oaxaca* Salsa (page 36)

2½ pounds baby spinach

2–3 tablespoons olive oil

2 small white onions or 6 green onions, including green parts, minced

¼ cup currants, plumped in hot water and drained

¼ cup pine nuts, toasted

Fine sea salt and freshly ground pepper

8 corn tortillas, warmed

½ cup crumbled goat cheese

1. Prepare the Tomatillo *Pasilla de Oaxaca* Salsa.

2. Rinse the spinach well and remove the stems. Put it in a large skillet pan with only the water clinging to the leaves. Cook over medium heat, turning as needed until wilted, just a few minutes. Drain well and set aside.

3. Add the oil to the now-empty pan and set over medium heat. Add the onions and sauté until tender, about 8 minutes. Add the spinach, currants, and pine nuts and sauté briefly to warm through. Season to taste with salt and pepper. Spoon the spinach onto the tortillas, drizzle with goat cheese and some Tomatillo *Pasilla de Oaxaca* Salsa, and serve warm or at room temperature.

Grilled SWEET POTATO *Tacos* with *Ancho* GLAZE and SPICY BLACK BEANS

YIELD: 8 TACOS

I am always looking for good fuel for running. Sweet potatoes have a ton of nutrients and are filling without being heavy. The Ancho-Maple Glaze adds a taste of fall. Add scrambled eggs for a healthy breakfast taco.

2 medium sweet potatoes (about 1 pound)

Vegetable oil to brush the grill,
    plus 1–2 teaspoons for the beans

1 cup rinsed and drained canned black beans

1 *habañero* chile

Ancho-Maple Glaze *(recipe follows)*

8 blue corn tortillas, warmed

2 cups grated cheese, such *Cotija*
    or *queso fresco*

Fine sea salt and freshly ground
    black pepper

¼ cup olive oil, plus oil to brush griddle

1 tablespoon *ancho* chile powder

ANCHO-MAPLE GLAZE

½ cup maple syrup

1 tablespoon Dijon mustard

1 tablespoon *ancho* chile powder

Fine sea salt and freshly ground pepper

1. In a large pot, bring enough lightly salted water to cover the potatoes to a boil. Add the potatoes, cover, and cook until just tender on the outside when pricked with the tip of a knife, about 12 minutes. Drain and, when cool enough to handle, peel and cut into ¼-inch-thick round slices.

2. Heat a grill or grill pan over high heat until hot. Brush with a little oil. Lay the potato slices on the grill and cook just until marked by the grill on both sides, turning once. Remove and set aside.

3. Meanwhile, in a food processor, puree the black beans and *habañero* with a little oil until almost smooth. Prepare the *Ancho*-Maple Glaze.

4. Heat a griddle or heavy skillet over medium-high heat.

5. For each tortilla, spoon about ¼ cup of beans over half of the tortilla, then top with ¼ cup of cheese and three slices of sweet potatoes. Season to taste with salt and pepper.

6. Fold each in half into a semicircle. Brush on a little oil and sprinkle with a little *ancho* chile powder. Griddle for 6 minutes or until crisp. Serve two per person and drizzle with *Ancho*-Maple Glaze.

Ancho-Maple Glaze

In a small bowl, stir together the maple syrup, mustard, and chile powder. Season to taste with salt and pepper.

SWISS CHARD, BEET, and GOAT CHEESE Tacos

YIELD: 12 TACOS

Beets are one of those love 'em or hate 'em foods. I'm in the first group, which is good because they are widely used in Mexican cuisine. I especially love their earthy-sweet taste when oven-roasted. Stir them together with tangy goat cheese and sautéed Swiss chard, and the combination makes an amazing vegetarian taco when drizzled with Spicy Mint Crema. Beets stain everything, so wear gloves.

8 medium beets, trimmed

2 tablespoons olive oil, plus oil to brush the beets

Spicy Mint *Crema* (recipe follows)

2 cloves garlic, minced

1 white onion, finely diced

2 bunches red Swiss chard, coarse stems removed and chopped

2 cups crumbled goat cheese

2 tablespoons finely chopped fresh oregano, preferably Mexican

Fine sea salt and freshly ground black pepper

12 corn tortillas, warmed

SPICY MINT *CREMA*

8 ounces *crema*, Greek yogurt, or crème fraîche

3 tablespoons freshly squeezed lemon juice

½ cup coarsely chopped mint leaves

¼ cup coarsely chopped cilantro

¼ cup coarsely chopped parsley leaves

2 cloves garlic

2 *serrano* chiles, seeded

Fine sea salt

1. Preheat the oven to 400 degrees. Brush the beets with a little oil, wrap tightly in aluminum foil, and roast until tender, from 40 minutes up to an hour or more, depending on the size. Check every 15 minutes until a knife tip can be easily inserted. Remove, cool, remove the skin, and cut into small cubes. Set aside.

2. Meanwhile, prepare the Spicy Mint *Crema*.

3. In a large skillet, heat 2 tablespoons of oil over medium heat. Add the garlic and onion, partially cover, and sweat for 3 minutes. Add the Swiss chard and cook for about 5 minutes, stirring occasionally, until the leaves are tender. Remove the pan from the heat, cool, and mix the chard with the beets, goat cheese, and oregano. Season to taste with salt and pepper.

4. Spoon the filling into the tortillas, drizzle with Spicy Mint *Crema,* and serve.

Spicy Mint *Crema*

In the jar of an electric blender, combine the *crema,* lemon juice, mint, cilantro, parsley, garlic, and *serranos;* blend well. Season to taste with salt.

Fried GREEN TOMATILLO Tacos with GREEN OLIVES and Chipotle RÉMOULADE

YIELD: 12 TACOS

My mom is from the South, and I love southern food. I always find a way to work it into my repertoire just for fun. If you're a fan of fried green tomatoes, I think you'll find battered and fried tangy tomatillos a new way to enjoy them, especially when garnished with green olives, watercress, and smoky-creamy Chipotle *Rémoulade.*

Chipotle Rémoulade *(recipe follows)*

1 cup all-purpose flour

1 teaspoon fine sea salt

½ teaspoon freshly ground black pepper

1 cup Tecate or other Mexican beer, at room temperature

2 pounds tomatillos, peeled, washed, cut into ¼-inch slices, and patted dry with paper towels

1 lime, cut in half crosswise

Vegetable oil for deep-frying

12 corn tortillas, warmed

1½ cups watercress, coarse stems removed

8 ounces green olives, sliced

8 ounces *queso fresco*, sliced

Lime wedges

Bottled hot pepper sauce, such as Cholula

CHIPOTLE RÉMOULADE

¼ cup mayonnaise, not light variety

¼ cup *chipotles en adobo*, finely diced

¼ cup crema, Greek yogurt, or *crème* fraîche

1 tablespoon chopped fresh tarragon leaves

Fine sea salt and freshly ground black pepper

1. Prepare the *Chipotle* Rémoulade.

2. In a bowl, whisk the flour, salt, and pepper together. Pour in the beer, whisking until the batter is smooth, and let it stand for 15 minutes.

3. Sprinkle the tomatillos with salt and pepper and squeeze on some lime juice. Let them stand for 15 minutes.

4. Heat the oven to 200 degrees. Line a baking sheet with paper towels.

5. In a medium-sized skillet, pour in enough oil to measure 2 inches deep. Attach a deep-fry thermometer and heat the oil to 350 degrees. Working in batches, dip the tomatillos into the batter, slide them into the oil, and fry until golden, about 4 minutes. Using a metal spatula, transfer the tomatillos to the baking sheet and keep warm in the oven. Repeat with the remaining tomatillos.

6. Fill each tortilla with two slices of tomatillo. Spoon on the *Chipotle* Rémoulade, some watercress, green olives, *queso fresco,* a squeeze of lime, and a dash of hot pepper sauce and serve.

Chipotle Rémoulade

In a bowl, whisk together the mayonnaise, *chipotles, crema,* and tarragon. Season to taste with salt and pepper.

Grilled SUMMER VEGETABLE Tacos

YIELD: 12 TACOS

Mexicans have a long-standing tradition of grilling outside, especially since many older rural houses don't have a kitchen. For these tasty vegetable tacos, I make my own version of chimichurri— the Argentine marinade typically used on steaks, which includes a little Maggi sauce and a bright red chile de árbol—which is brushed and brush it onto the vegetables as they are grilled or roasted in the oven. The chimichurri sauce is very popular in Mexico as well. The recipe is very flexible: Change the vegetables to suit your own taste. If your grill has wide-spaced grates, you can prevent the pieces from falling into the fire by cutting the vegetables into large pieces; after cooking, cut them into smaller cubes.

Maggi Chimichurri Sauce *(recipe follows)*

½ cup *Pico de Gallo* (page 39)

2 chayotes, cut into medium-sized cubes

2 red onions, cut in eighths

2 *poblano* chiles, seeded and cut into medium-sized cubes

2 red bell peppers, seeded and cut into medium-sized cubes

2 medium zucchini, trimmed and cut into medium-sized cubes

Fine sea salt and freshly ground black pepper

2 cups shredded romaine lettuce

1½ tablespoons extra-virgin olive oil

½ tablespoon red wine vinegar

8 corn tortillas, warmed

½ cup crumbled *queso fresco*

1. Prepare the Maggi Chimichurri Sauce and *Pico de Gallo*. Heat a grill or preheat the oven to 425 degrees.

2. Toss the vegetables with a little of the Maggi Chimichurri Sauce, turning to coat evenly. Lay them on the grill and cook until tender and nicely browned, about 15 minutes, turning every 10 minutes. Or transfer them to a large roasting pan and roast in the oven until tender, turning every 10 minutes.

3. Remove, spoon a generous tablespoon of the Chimichurri Sauce over the vegetables, season to taste with salt and pepper, and toss.

4. While the vegetables roast, toss the romaine with the oil and vinegar and season with salt and pepper to taste.

5. Spoon the vegetables into the tortillas, top with romaine and *queso fresco,* and finish with a spoonful of *Pico de Gallo*. Pass extra Maggi Chimichurri Sauce at the table.

MAGGI CHIMICHURRI SAUCE

1 cup blended oil
   (see the introduction), divided

2 tablespoons minced garlic

½ *chile de árbol*, crushed

2 tablespoons sherry vinegar

1 tablespoon freshly squeezed lime juice

1 tablespoon Maggi sauce

¼ tablespoon dried oregano,
   preferably Mexican

Fine sea salt

2 tablespoons flat-leaf parsley,
   cut into chiffonade

Maggi Chimichurri Sauce

In a skillet, heat a tablespoon of the oil over medium-high heat and sauté the garlic and chile together until light golden brown. Add the vinegar, lime juice, Maggi, and oregano; simmer for 10 minutes to combine the flavors. Add salt, if needed. Remove, cool, and stir in the parsley.

VEGETARIAN *Tacos*

Smoke-Roasted ROOT VEGETABLE Tacos

YIELD: 12 TACOS

If you have a chimney or smoker, these roasted root vegetables make a comforting yet sophisticated taco filling. Enjoy them with friends over a nice cold porter or dark toasted lager. Alternatively, you can oven-roast or grill root vegetables until nicely caramelized and use them in tacos.

2 large carrots, cut into 2-inch chunks

2 medium unpeeled russet potatoes, cut into 2-inch chunks

2 medium unpeeled rutabagas, cut into 2-inch chunks

¼ cup extra-virgin olive oil, plus more for drizzling

Fine sea salt and freshly ground black pepper

Roasted Tomato *Chile de Árbol* Salsa (page 34)

12 corn tortillas, warmed

¾ cup crumbled *Cotija* cheese

2 tablespoons chopped flat-leaf parsley, for garnish

1. Toss the carrots, potatoes, and rutabagas with the oil and season with salt and pepper to taste. Transfer to an 8 x 12-inch piece of heavy-duty aluminum foil or a disposable aluminum pan.

2. Fill a charcoal chimney with briquettes, set the chimney on the bottom grill grate, and light. Or prepare a fire in your smoker. For a gas grill, turn half the burners to medium.

3. When the coals are ready, dump them into the bottom of your grill and spread them evenly across half. Scatter wood chips on the hot coals or place them in a metal container as close as possible to a burner on a gas grill. Place the vegetables on the indirect-heat side and close the lid. Smoke at 350 degrees until the potatoes are tender and the vegetables have a good, smoky aroma, 45 to 60 minutes.

4. Meanwhile, prepare the Roasted Tomato *Chile de Árbol* Salsa.

5. When the vegetables are cooked, drizzle on the remaining oil, and divide the mixture among the tortillas. Add a little *Cotija* cheese and parsley along with a spoonful of Roasted Tomato *Chile de Árbol* Salsa to each taco and serve.

ZUCCHINI, BLACK BEAN, and CORN TACOS with Salsa Verde

YIELD: 16 TACOS

This very Mexican blend of zucchini, black beans, and corn is another popular Dos Caminos side dish that makes a terrific vegetarian taco filling with queso fresco *and* Salsa Verde *added. Pile it cold on top of shredded lettuce for a healthy summer salad.*

Salsa Verde (page 33)

2 tablespoons olive oil

3 cloves garlic, minced

1 large white onion, chopped

4 medium zucchini, trimmed and diced

2 Thai chiles, seeds removed, if desired, and very thinly sliced

1 *poblano* chile, diced

2 cups canned black beans, rinsed and drained

1 cup corn kernels

1 teaspoon Maggi sauce

Fine sea salt

16 corn tortillas, warmed

1 cup crumbled *queso fresco*

1. Prepare the *Salsa Verde*.

2. In a large skillet, heat the oil over medium-high heat. Add the garlic and onion and sauté until translucent, stirring frequently. Add the zucchini, Thai chiles, and *poblano* pepper and sauté until just tender but still slightly crisp.

3. Stir in the beans, corn, and Maggi sauce; heat through. Season to taste with salt.

4. Spoon the mixture into the tortillas, drizzle on *queso fresco* and *Salsa Verde,* and serve.

FISH AND SEAFOOD
Tacos

Salt-Crusted ROASTED SALMON *Tacos* with BLACK BEAN, CORN, *and* MANGO SALSA

YIELD: 8 TACOS

Baking salmon in a salt crust, as you'll do with the fillets in these tacos,
is a technique I grabbed while traveling in Turkey. This ensures fish that is moist and flavorful
but not salty. It's perfectly partnered with colorful Black Bean, Corn, and Mango Salsa.
The tacos are served in tortillas and accompanied by an arugula salad tossed with
a sprightly Lime Cumin Vinaigrette. Enjoy with spiked cider or a dry chenin blanc from Baja.

Black Bean, Corn, and Mango Salsa
(recipe follows)

Lime Cumin Crème Fraîche (recipe follows)

Lime Cumin Vinaigrette (recipe follows)

8 corn tortillas

8 (3-ounce) pieces skinless salmon fillets

4–6 cups kosher or coarse sea salt

¼ cup cilantro leaves

1½ cups baby arugula

2 teaspoons toasted sesame seeds

6 ounces goat cheese, crumbled

8 lime wedges

1. Prepare the Black Bean, Corn, and Mango Salsa, Lime Cumin Crème Fraîche, and Lime Cumin Vinaigrette. Set aside.

2. Preheat the oven to 450 degrees.

3. In a flat pan large enough to hold the salmon fillets in a single layer, spread half of the salt over the bottom. Arrange the salmon on top of the salt and cover with the remaining salt, packing it firmly on the fish. Bake for about 8 minutes. The salmon should be pink and moist in the center. Test by inserting a knife tip through the salt and into a piece of fish to check. Remove the salmon from the oven and cool slightly.

4. Using a spatula, lift off the salt crust. Break up the salmon with your fingers and place it in a bowl. Drizzle with a little vinaigrette. Add the cilantro leaves.

5. On each dinner plate, put a tortilla. Top with ⅓ cup Black Bean, Corn, and Mango Salsa, then divide the salmon among the tortillas.

6. In a bowl, lightly dress the arugula with the remaining vinaigrette. Add the sesame seeds and toss. Place a small mound of greens on each tortilla and sprinkle with goat cheese. Drizzle with the Lime Cumin Crème Fraîche, add a lime wedge, and serve. Pass extra salsa at the table.

2 tablespoons olive oil

2 cloves garlic, minced

2 green onions, including most of
the green parts, chopped

1 small red onion, diced

1 small red bell pepper, seeds and
membranes removed and diced

1 cup corn kernels

1 teaspoon freshly squeezed lemon juice

1 teaspoon ground cumin

¼ teaspoon ground cardamom

½ teaspoon soy sauce

2 cups cooked or canned black beans,
rinsed well and drained

1 small mango, peeled and diced
[see the sidebar on page 31]

4 fresh basil leaves, cut in chiffonade

¼ cup chopped cilantro

3–4 tablespoons extra-virgin olive oil

Fine sea salt and freshly ground
black pepper

LIME CUMIN CRÈME FRAÎCHE

½ cup crème fraîche

1 tablespoon freshly squeezed lime juice

1 teaspoon grated lime zest

½ teaspoon ground cumin

Fine sea salt

LIME CUMIN VINAIGRETTE

¼ cup red wine vinegar

1 tablespoon freshly squeezed lime juice

½ teaspoon ground cumin

Fine sea salt and freshly ground
black pepper

⅓ cup extra-virgin olive oil

Black Bean, Corn, and Mango Salsa

1. In a large shallow skillet, heat the oil over medium-high heat. Add the garlic, green and red onions, bell pepper, corn, lemon juice, cumin, cardamom, and soy.

2. When the vegetables are tender, stir in the black beans, mango, basil, and cilantro; remove from the heat. Add the olive oil and cool. Season to taste with salt and freshly ground black pepper.

Lime Cumin Crème Fraîche

In a small bowl, stir the crème fraîche, lime juice and zest, and cumin together. Season to taste with salt and use immediately.

Lime Cumin Vinaigrette

In a small bowl, combine the vinegar, lime juice, cumin, salt, and pepper to taste, mixing well. Whisk in the oil until emulsified. Set aside.

BAJA-STYLE FISH *Tacos* with WHITE SAUCE

YIELD: 16 TACOS

Just south of the California border, in Baja, I discovered countless different kinds of fried cod tacos and I never tired of eating them. Often they're topped with seasoned mayonnaise or what is called "white sauce" in Mexico. This version is typical of those found at numerous street stands in Mexico. Most often they're prepared with shark, but any firm white-fleshed fish will work. Cornstarch in the batter helps it adhere to the fish. Garlic salt is a commonly used seasoning in Mexico. Other familiar garnishes you might use include shredded lettuce, julienned radishes, and thinly sliced chiles. You might also serve these with pickled jalapeños.

1 cup mayonnaise, not light variety

¼ cup milk

¼ cup freshly squeezed lemon juice

1 teaspoon garlic salt

Blended oil for frying

1 cup all-purpose flour

½ cup cornstarch

1 teaspoon garlic powder

1 cup ice-cold Mexican beer, such as Tecate

8 flour or corn tortillas, warmed

1½ pounds boneless cod,
    cut into 2-inch pieces and patted dry

½ teaspoon fine sea salt

2 cups finely shredded white cabbage

2 limes, cut into wedges

1. In a small bowl, whisk together the mayonnaise, milk, lemon juice, and garlic salt. Set aside.

2. Preheat a deep-fat fryer or deep pot filled halfway with oil until the oil measures 375 degrees on an instant-read thermometer.

3. Meanwhile, in a medium bowl, sift the flour, cornstarch, and garlic powder together; whisk in the beer. Warm the tortillas.

4. Season the fish pieces with salt and dip into the batter, letting any excess drip back into the bowl. Add to the hot oil, taking care not to crowd them, and cook until golden brown and cooked through, about 3 minutes. Remove with a slotted spoon to paper towels to drain.

5. For each tortilla, put on a piece of fish, drizzle with white sauce, top with a little shredded cabbage, and squeeze on lime juice to taste.

Grilled MAHIMAHI Tacos, Baja-Style, with PINEAPPLE Habañero HOT SAUCE

YIELD: 8 TACOS

While Baja is famous for beer-battered fried fish tacos, an equally delicious and lighter version can be made by grilling the firm-fleshed, mild-tasting mahimahi and serving it on tortillas. What makes this dish so appealing is the contrast of textures and tastes: the crunchy Citrus-Cucumber Slaw, creamy Roasted Jalapeño Lime Aioli, warm tortillas, and smoky grilled fish.

Other fish suitable for these tacos include red snapper and hake, a super-inexpensive and, I believe, underrated option. If you prefer traditional deep-fried tacos, see the recipe on page 111.

Citrus-Cucumber Slaw (page 63)

Charred Pineapple *Habañero* Hot Sauce
(recipe follows)

Roasted *Jalapeño* Lime Aioli
(recipe follows), for drizzling

8 (3-ounce) mahimahi fillets, blotted dry

2 tablespoons blended oil

Fine sea salt and freshly ground
black pepper

8 corn tortillas

4 limes, quartered

**CHARRED PINEAPPLE *HABAÑERO*
HOT SAUCE**

2–3 (½-inch-thick) slices fresh pineapple,
cored

1 teaspoon blended oil, plus oil to brush
the pineapple slices

1 small white onion, coarsely chopped

½ cup shredded pineapple
in pineapple juice

1 *habañero* chile, chopped

¼ cup rice vinegar

Fine sea salt and freshly ground
black pepper

1. Make the Citrus-Cucumber Slaw, Charred Pineapple *Habañero* Hot Sauce, and Roasted *Jalapeño* Lime Aioli.

2. Preheat a grill or a grill pan.

3. Brush the fillets with oil and season with salt and pepper. Lay them on the grill and cook until the flesh is charred, 3 to 4 minutes per side, turning once.

4. Quickly warm the tortillas on the grill. Cut each piece of fish in half after it's grilled. Place a piece of fish on each tortilla, garnish with a little of the Citrus-Cucumber Slaw, and drizzle each taco with a tablespoon of the Pineapple *Habañero* Hot Sauce.

5. Fold the tortillas in half. Place two tacos on each plate, liberally drizzle with Roasted *Jalapeño* Lime Aioli, and serve warm with lime quarters.

Charred Pineapple *Habañero* Hot Sauce

Heat a grill to very hot. Lightly brush the pineapple with a little oil and grill for 2 minutes, turning once. Remove, cool, and cut into fine cubes. In a small saucepan, heat the teaspoon of oil over medium heat. Stir in the onion and cook until translucent. Add the shredded pineapple, *habañero,* and vinegar and cook for 4 minutes to blend the flavors. Transfer to the jar of an electric blender and puree until smooth. Scrape into a bowl, add the diced pineapple, season to taste with salt and pepper, and set aside.

6 *jalapeño* peppers

2 cups mayonnaise, not light variety

Zest of 2 large limes

¼ cup freshly squeezed lime juice

Fine sea salt and freshly ground
black pepper

Roasted *Jalapeño* Lime Aioli

Roast the *jalapeños* on a hot grill until the skins are browned and blistered, 6 to 8 minutes, then seed and dice them. In a bowl, whisk the *jalapeños,* mayonnaise, lime zest, and lime juice together. Season to taste with salt and pepper. Use liberally.

BEER-BATTERED
Fried Fish

YIELD: 8 TACOS

*If you still crave the crispiness of fried fish rather than the grilled,
here's a recipe for making it with mahimahi. It has all the same toppings as the grilled version,
so you could grill some fish and fry some fish, and let everyone pick and choose.*

Citrus-Cucumber Slaw (page 63)

Charred Pineapple Habanero Hot Sauce
(page 102)

Roasted *Jalapeno* Lime Aioli
(recipe follows), **for drizzling**

1½ cups all-purpose flour

1 tablespoon ancho chile powder

1 tablespoon kosher salt

1 teaspoon baking powder

1 large egg

1 (12-ounce) can Tecate or other light
beer, preferably Mexican, very cold

Blended oil for frying

2 pounds mahimahi steaks,
cut into 4-inch-wide strips

8 corn tortillas

4 limes, quartered

1. In a medium-sized mixing bowl, combine the flour, chile powder, salt, and baking powder; mix. In another bowl, beat the egg until smooth and then stir in the beer.

2. Whisk the dry ingredients into the liquids, stirring until smooth.

3. Meanwhile, in a large, deep skillet, pour in enough oil to measure 1 inch deep. Heat the oil over high heat until hot, about 350 degrees on an instant-read thermometer.

4. Dip the pieces of fish into the batter, letting the excess fall back into the bowl, and fry until golden brown, about 4 minutes; turn and cook the second side for the same amount of time. Remove the fish with a spatula or slotted spoon, and blot on paper towels to remove excess oil.

5. Divide the fish among the tortillas. For each taco, garnish with a little of the Citrus-Cucumber Slaw, and drizzle each taco with a tablespoon of the Pineapple Habañero Hot Sauce.

6. Fold the tortillas in half. Place two tacos on each plate, liberally drizzle with Roasted *Jalapeño* Lime Aioli, and serve warm with lime quarters.

BAJA-STYLE COD *Tacos* with **ROASTED TOMATO** *Rémoulade*

YIELD: 8 TACOS

These crispy cod finger tacos topped with Guacamole, Red Cabbage Fennel Apple Slaw, and smoky Roasted Tomato Rémoulade are synonymous with Baja cuisine. Shark is typically the fish of choice for tacos. It's plentiful in all the fish market stalls in Ensenada, for example. I'm sure you'll use this rémoulade on many tacos and the cabbage slaw is a favorite accompaniment for dishes like tacos and burritos, as well as almost any sandwich. This colorful blend is far more appealing than the routine version that often gets pushed to the side of the plate.

The sauce, slaw, and prep for the Guacamole may all be done several hours ahead, but mash the avocados just before serving. Although I think beer in the batter makes delicious tacos, you can substitute club soda with a little Old Bay seasoning added to bump up the taste.

Roasted Tomato Rémoulade (recipe follows)

Red Cabbage Fennel Apple Slaw (recipe follows)

Guacamole (page 44)

2 (12-ounce) cans Tecate beer

2 cups all-purpose flour

1 teaspoon fine sea salt

Blended oil for deep-frying

8 flour tortillas

8 (2-ounce) pieces cod,
    about 3 x 1 x 1 inches each, patted dry

Freshly ground black pepper

1. Prepare the Roasted Tomato Rémoulade, Red Cabbage Fennel Apple Slaw, and Guacamole.

2. In a large bowl, stir the beer, flour, and salt together until smooth.

3. In a deep skillet, pour in enough oil to measure about 2 inches deep and heat over high heat until the oil measures 375 degrees on an instant-read thermometer.

4. Heat the oven to 400 degrees. Wrap the tortillas in a clean towel or aluminum foil and heat until warm, about 5 minutes.

5. Season the fish with salt and pepper. Dip the cod into the batter, letting extra batter run off, and add them to the oil, taking care not to crowd the pieces. Cook until golden brown and crispy all over, about 4 minutes, turning if needed. Using a slotted spoon, remove the fish to paper towels to drain. Season to taste with salt and pepper.

6. On each tortilla, spread a tablespoon of Guacamole, topping this with a piece of fish and about ¼ cup of slaw. Drizzle with Roasted Tomato Rémoulade and serve with refried beans and red rice, if desired. Pass extra rémoulade at the table.

ROASTED TOMATO RÉMOULADE

2 Roma tomatoes, split lengthwise

1 egg yolk, at room temperature

2 teaspoons freshly squeezed lemon juice

½ teaspoon Dijon mustard

½ teaspoon rice vinegar

½ cup blended oil

1 teaspoon smoked hot paprika,
  such as *Pimentón de la Vera*

1 teaspoon chopped fresh tarragon leaves

Salt and freshly ground pepper

RED CABBAGE FENNEL APPLE SLAW

1 *serrano* chile, seeded and
  very thinly sliced

1 Granny Smith apple, cored and julienned

1 small fennel bulb, trimmed, cored,
  and julienned

1 small carrot, julienned

½ small head red cabbage,
  cored and julienned

½ small red onion, julienned

¼ cup thinly sliced cilantro

3 ounces white vinegar

¼ cup mayonnaise, not light variety

½ tablespoon sugar

Fine sea salt and freshly ground
  black pepper

Roasted Tomato Rémoulade

1. Preheat the oven to 325 degrees.

2. Roast the tomatoes on a sheet pan, cut-side down, for 12 minutes, or until dry. Coarsely chop and set aside.

3. In a food processor, combine the egg yolk, lemon juice, mustard, and vinegar; process for 1 minute. With the motor running, slowly drizzle in the oil, beginning with a drop at a time and gradually increasing the flow as the mixture emulsifies. Add the tomatoes, paprika, and tarragon and pulse until combined but not completely smooth. Season to taste with salt and pepper. Scrape into a bowl and set aside. If made several hours ahead, refrigerate until serving.

Red Cabbage Fennel Apple Slaw

YIELD: 8 GENEROUS SERVINGS

In a large bowl, combine the chile, apple, fennel, carrot, cabbage, onion, cilantro, vinegar, mayonnaise, and sugar; mix well. Season to taste with salt and pepper. Cover and refrigerate until served.

GRILLED RED SNAPPER TACOS
Yucatán-Style

YIELD: 8 TACOS

*Mexico's Yucatán was once isolated from the rest of the country by rough terrain and poor roads.
As a result, Yucatecan cooking absorbed flavors from the Europeans, Cubans, and people
of New Orleans who came through the ports. Fresh seafood is plentiful in the region.
In these tacos, along with the fresh citrus juices, the marinade includes achiote,
a paste of Mayan origins that turns foods bright yellow-orange from ground annatto seeds
mixed with garlic, vinegar, spices like cinnamon and allspice, and salt.*

Mango Avocado Slaw *(recipe follows)*

White Salsa *(recipe follows)*

3 tablespoons *achiote* paste

½ cup freshly squeezed orange juice

½ cup freshly squeezed lime juice

¼ cup freshly squeezed grapefruit juice

2 tablespoons olive oil

2 cloves garlic, finely minced

Fine sea salt and freshly ground
    black pepper

2 pounds red snapper fillets

8 corn tortillas

½ small head red cabbage, shredded

Leaves from 1 bunch fresh cilantro

Lime wedges, for garnish

1. Prepare the Mango Avocado Slaw and White Salsa.

2. Preheat a charcoal or gas grill to medium heat.

3. In a small bowl, break the *achiote* paste into small pieces, then whisk it together with the citrus juices, olive oil, garlic, and salt and pepper. Brush on both sides of the fish and season with salt and pepper.

4. Grill the fish until golden brown and just cooked through, about 4 minutes per side. Remove from the grill, let rest 5 minutes, and flake into large pieces with a fork.

5. Place about 3 ounces of fish into a corn tortilla and garnish with cabbage, cilantro, Mango Avocado Slaw, and a drizzle of White Salsa. Serve with lime wedges on the side. Pass extra salsa at the table.

2 ripe avocados, preferably Hass variety,
   peeled, pitted, and diced

1 firm, ripe mango, peeled, seeded,
   and thinly sliced

½ small red onion, finely sliced

3 *serrano* chiles, finely sliced

Juice of 2 limes

2 tablespoons olive oil

1 teaspoon agave syrup

Fine sea salt and freshly ground
   black pepper

¼ cup cilantro leaves, cut in chiffonade

WHITE SALSA

4 ripe Roma tomatoes, seeded and diced

2 cloves garlic, finely diced

2 *serrano* chiles, finely diced

½ small red onion, finely diced

2 tablespoons Greek yogurt

2 tablespoons olive oil

1 tablespoon rice vinegar

Fine sea salt

Mango Avocado Slaw

Combine the avocados, mango, onion, chiles, lime juice, oil, agave, and salt and pepper in a medium serving bowl. Before serving, add the cilantro and toss to blend.

White Salsa

In a medium bowl, combine the tomatoes, garlic, chiles, and onion.
In a separate bowl, whisk together the yogurt, oil, vinegar, and salt to taste.
Combine the tomato mixture with the dressing.

LIME-MARINATED TUNA *Tacos with* PAPAYA, MUSTARD, *and* ROSEMARY SALSA

YIELD: 8 TACOS

Diced papaya and red onion tossed with lime juice and mustard are a sexy accent for briefly sautéed tuna, tomatoes, and onions in these tacos. Papayas' intense perfume and luscious, sweet orange-hued flesh reputedly led Christopher Columbus to call them the "fruit of the angels." Most varieties weigh about a pound. The peppery-tasting black seeds inside are edible.

Papaya, Mustard, and Rosemary Salsa
(recipe follows)

8 flour tortillas

1 pound yellowfin tuna

1 cup freshly squeezed lime juice

1 tablespoon blended oil

4 Roma tomatoes, cored, seeded, and julienned

1 small red onion, diced

Fine sea salt and freshly ground black pepper

1 tablespoon chopped cilantro

PAPAYA, MUSTARD, AND ROSEMARY SALSA

1 large ripe papaya (about 1 pound), peeled, seeded, and cut into ½-inch dice

1 small red onion, diced

1 tablespoon Dijon mustard

1 tablespoon freshly squeezed lime juice

Leaves from 1 sprig fresh rosemary, minced

1. Prepare the Papaya, Mustard, and Rosemary Salsa.

2. Cut the tuna into ½-inch cubes and transfer to a non-reactive bowl. Pour on the lime juice, mix, and marinate for no longer than 15 minutes. Drain the liquid and reserve.

3. Meanwhile, warm the tortillas and place them in a folded napkin or towel to keep warm.

4. In a large saucepan, heat the oil over high heat until hot. Add the tuna and stir just to coat. Add the tomatoes and onion; season with salt and pepper. Pour in the reserved lime juice, add the cilantro, turn off the heat, and let the pan sit for a couple of seconds until the fish is cooked to the desired temperature. (It will cook very quickly.) Spoon the mixture onto the warm tortillas, top with Papaya, Mustard, and Rosemary Salsa, and serve.

Papaya, Mustard, and Rosemary Salsa

In a bowl, stir the papaya, onion, mustard, lime juice, and rosemary together. Cover and refrigerate for at least half an hour.

TUNA *Tacos with* LIME AIOLI *and* HONEYDEW JICAMA SLAW

YIELD: 16 TACOS

Bright summer flavors fill in these grilled tuna tacos. The fish is topped with Honeydew Jicama Slaw and balanced with mildly peppery watercress in a Lime Aioli. Once the toppings are made— a day before, if you like—the final assembly is very easy and quick.

Jicama, also known as a "Mexican potato," is a crunchy tuber that sort of crosses a potato with an apple is more of a textured carrier of other flavors. Generally, it's served raw and crunchy.

Honeydew Jicama Slaw *(recipe follows)*

2 *jalapeños*, roasted and seeded

Finely grated zest of 2 limes

2 cups mayonnaise, not light variety

¼ cup olive oil

2 tablespoons red wine vinegar

Fine sea salt and freshly ground
   black pepper

1 cup watercress, thick stems removed

16 flour tortillas

2 pounds sushi-grade tuna, cut into
   16 (2-ounce) portions

Blended oil

HONEYDEW JICAMA SLAW

1½ cups peeled and julienned
   honeydew melon

1½ cups peeled and julienned jicama

4 *jalapeños*, seeded and julienned

Zest of 2 lemons

1 tablespoon agave nectar

1. Prepare the Honeydew Jicama Slaw.

2. For the Lime Aioli: In a bowl, combine the *jalapeños,* lime zest, and mayonnaise.

3. In a small bowl, beat the oil and vinegar together, seasoning with salt and pepper. Add the watercress, toss, cover, and set aside.

4. Heat a grill or heavy skillet until hot. Heat the tortillas and put two on each of eight large plates.

5. Brush a grill, grill pan, or large heavy skillet with a little oil and cook the tuna until rare, about 1½ minutes per side, turning once. Remove and cut across the grain into thin slices.

6. Spoon the watercress on the tortillas, lay the sliced tuna in layers on top, add the Honeydew Jicama Slaw, and finish with a dollop of Lime Aioli.

Honeydew Jicama Slaw

In a bowl, stir together the honeydew, jicama, *jalapeños,* lemon zest, and agave nectar. Cover and refrigerate.

TUNA *in* CHAYOTE *Taco Shells* *with* TOMATO *Serrano* SALSITA

YIELD: 8 TACOS

Sushi-grade tuna tacos are a huge favorite at Dos Caminos, and we do them in many ways. In this version, Chayote Taco Shells are my contemporary approach to traditional tortillas. The fish is quickly put in a mildly spicy soy marinade and finally topped with a tangy-sweet Tomato Serrano Salsita.

Enjoy these tacos with a sophisticated glass of dry white wine from Northern Baja.

¾ cup Tomato *Serrano* Salsita (recipe follows)

8 Chayote Taco Shells (recipe follows)

½ cup soy sauce

¼ cup crushed red pepper

¼ cup flaky sea salt, such as Maldon

2 tablespoons dried oregano, preferably Mexican

Leaves from 10 sprigs cilantro

8 (3-ounce) pieces sushi-grade tuna

1 avocado, preferably Hass variety

TOMATO *SERRANO* SALSITA

1 tablespoon blended oil

2 *serrano* chiles, thinly sliced

2 cloves garlic, slivered

½ white onion, cut into small dice

6 tablespoons sugar

¼ cup balsamic vinegar

2 tablespoons rice vinegar

6 Roma tomatoes, cored, seeded, and cut into small dice

8 basil leaves, cut into chiffonade

Leaves from 8 sprigs cilantro, cut into chiffonade

Fine sea salt

1. Make the Tomato *Serrano* Salsita and Chayote Taco Shells.

2. In a small bowl, mix the soy sauce, red pepper, salt, oregano, and cilantro leaves together. Slice each piece of tuna into three equal finger-length pieces, each weighing about 1 ounce. Cover with the marinade, turning to coat evenly, and let them stand for at least 1 minute.

3. Peel and cut the avocado into slices. Put a piece of tuna and a slice of avocado in each Chayote Taco Shell. Spoon on the Tomato *Serrano* Salsita and serve.

Tomato *Serrano* Salsita

1. In a medium skillet, heat the oil over medium heat. Stir in the chiles, garlic, and onion, partially cover, and sweat for about 2 minutes. Add the sugar and let it slightly caramelize, 2 to 3 minutes.

2. Stir in the vinegars, raise the heat to high, and reduce the liquid by half. Stir in the tomatoes and remove the pan from the heat to cool. When cool, add the herbs and season to taste with salt. Transfer to a bowl and refrigerate. The mixture should be a little thick.

CHAYOTE TACO SHELLS

2 large chayotes

Blended oil, for frying

1 cup all-purpose flour seasoned with salt and pepper

2 large eggs, beaten

1 cup panko bread crumbs

Chayote Taco Shells

1. Peel and slice the chayotes crosswise into ¼-inch slices and pat dry.

2. Pour enough oil into a skillet to measure 2 inches deep and heat to 350 degrees when measured on a candy thermometer. Turn the oven to warm.

3. Put the flour, eggs, and bread crumbs into three flat bowls. Coat a slice of chayote with flour, patting to remove any excess. Dip the slice into the egg, letting any excess run off, then coat with panko. Slide each slice into the hot oil and cook until golden brown, 2 to 3 minutes. Transfer to a sheet pan and keep in the oven.

CHEF'S TIPS:

Chayote, also known as an alligator pear, is a squash-like green fruit that resembles a pear and is native to Mexico. Remove its firm skin with a sharp paring knife or vegetable peeler. When cooked, the exterior of these taco "shells" is crisp and crunchy while the interior is soft.

VEGETARIAN *Tacos*

TUNA TACOS *in* LETTUCE LEAVES *á la Flaca*

YIELD: 12 TACOS

In Mexico, a very slender, pretty young woman might be called la flaca—*the skinny girl. In these tacos, thinly sliced, sesame-crusted yellowfin tuna is wrapped in lettuce leaves rather than taco shells and topped with a fetching combination of Black Bean* Pico de Gallo *and* Hot Papaya Mango *Salsa. You can make the Papaya Mango Salsa a day or two ahead and refrigerate it.*

Black Bean *Pico de Gallo* (page 41)

Hot Papaya Mango Salsa *(recipe follows)*

6 (5-ounce) pieces yellowfin tuna

Fine sea salt and freshly ground
  black pepper

2 tablespoons sesame seeds

Blended oil

12 large leaves red-leaf lettuce

HOT PAPAYA MANGO SALSA

1 ripe mango, peeled and diced
  (see page 000)

1 ripe papaya, peeled, seeded, and diced

1 large red bell pepper, seeds and
  membranes removed and diced

1 *habañero* chile, minced

1/2 red onion, diced

2 tablespoons chopped cilantro

2 tablespoons rice vinegar

1 tablespoon honey

1 teaspoon *ancho* chile powder

Fine sea salt and freshly ground
  black pepper

1. Make the Black Bean *Pico de Gallo* and Hot Papaya Mango Salsa.

2. Season the tuna with salt and pepper and roll in the sesame seeds to coat.

3. Coat the bottom of a large skillet with oil and heat over medium-high heat until it shimmers. Place the tuna pieces in the skillet and sear for 2 minutes on each side for medium-rare, turning once. Remove and, using a sharp slicing knife, cut each piece across the grain into four slices.

4. Put a lettuce leaf on each plate and top with 1 tablespoon Black Bean *Pico de Gallo*. Add a slice of tuna and a generous tablespoon of Hot Papaya Mango Salsa on top. Pass the remaining salsas at the table.

Hot Papaya Mango Salsa

In a medium bowl, mix the mango, papaya, red bell pepper, *habañero*, onion, cilantro, vinegar, honey, and *ancho* chile powder. Season to taste with salt and pepper, cover, and set aside.

SMOKED SWORDFISH TACOS WITH
Pasilla de Oaxaca VINAIGRETTE

YIELD: 8 TACOS

Smoking swordfish over hardwood chips imparts a hint of charcoal flavor to the dense, meaty steaks. For these tacos, the fish is gently shredded and simply dressed with olive oil, lime, onion, and cilantro. The fish market in Baja is known for its smoked tuna, which would be great here, too.

1¼ pounds (1-inch-thick) swordfish steaks

Pasilla de Oaxaca Vinaigrette *(recipe follows)*

⅓ cup extra-virgin olive oil

3 tablespoons freshly squeezed lime juice

½ half red onion, very thinly sliced

¼ cup cilantro leaves

2 cups watercress, coarse stems removed

1½ cups julienned jicama

3 tangerines, peeled and separated into segments

1 large ripe avocado, peeled, pitted, and pureed with ½ teaspoon salt

PASILLA DE OAXACA VINAIGRETTE

5 *pasilla de Oaxaca* chiles, stemmed, seeded, toasted, and rehydrated

1 clove garlic

¾ cup rice vinegar

1¼ cups vegetable or olive oil or a blend of both

Fine sea salt

1. Prepare a smoker for hot smoking by soaking and then igniting the hardwood chips and regulating the temperature so the temperature will remain between 240 and 250 degrees.

2. Smoke the fish until the flesh is flaky and cooked through, 1 to 1¼ hours. Remove the fish, gently shred it, and refrigerate until you're ready to serve.

3. While the fish is smoking, make the *Pasilla de Oaxaca* Vinaigrette. Set aside.

4. In a small bowl, toss the swordfish with the olive oil, lime juice, onion, and cilantro leaves.

5. Mix about two-thirds of the *Pasilla de Oaxaca* Vinaigrette with the watercress, jicama, and tangerine segments, turning gently and adding more, if needed.

6. Spread a small dab of avocado puree in the center of each tortilla. Spoon on the watercress salad and top with the swordfish mixture.

Pasilla de Oaxaca Vinaigrette

In the jar of an electric blender, combine the chiles, garlic, and vinegar; puree until smooth. With the motor running, slowly add the oil. Scrape the dressing into a bowl, season to taste with salt, and set aside.

FISH *and* SEAFOOD *Tacos*

121

CRAB Salpicón Tacos

YIELD: 8 TACOS

In Mexico, foods en salpicón *refers to a mixture of diced or finely chopped pickled vegetables and a protein. For this lively, refreshing taco, crab is combined with celery, onion, carrot, radishes, and a* serrano *chile. Enjoy any extra vegetables for up to 4 days.*

Chipotle Aioli (page 47)

Pickled Vegetables *(recipe follows)*

1 pound lump crabmeat,
 picked to remove any cartilage

3 tablespoons olive oil

Juice of 1 lime

Fine sea salt and freshly ground
 black pepper

8 corn tortillas, fried until crisp

4 cups field greens or baby lettuces

½ cup cilantro leaves, for garnish

PICKLED VEGETABLES

2 cups red wine vinegar

½ cup sugar

½ tablespoon each coriander, allspice,
 mustard seed, and black peppercorns

½ *chile de árbol*

½ cinnamon stick, preferably
 Mexican *canela*

2 medium stalks celery, sliced on
 the bias into 2-inch lengths

1 carrot, sliced into ¼-inch circles

½ red onion, very thinly sliced

½ *serrano* chile, seeded and thinly sliced

½ cup very thinly sliced radishes

1. Prepare the *Chipotle* Aioli and the Pickled Vegetables.

2. In a bowl, combine the crab, aioli, oil, and lime juice. Season to taste with salt and pepper and gently mix. Set aside.

3. With a slotted spoon, transfer about ½ cup of pickled vegetables to a bowl and combine them with the crab mixture, adding slightly more if desired.

4. Put a tortilla on each large plate. Using your hands, gently form the lettuce into a nest and lay it on each taco. Spoon the crab-vegetable mixture in the center, garnish with cilantro leaves, and serve.

Pickled Vegetables

1. In a small non-reactive saucepan, combine the vinegar, sugar, coriander, allspice, mustard seed, peppercorns, *chile de árbol,* and cinnamon stick. Bring to a boil over high heat. Remove the pan from the heat and let it stand for 10 minutes.

2. Meanwhile, in another non-reactive bowl, combine the celery, carrot, onion, *serrano* chile, and radishes. Strain the liquid over the vegetables, cover, and refrigerate until well chilled. They can be used after 2 hours or for up to 4 days.

GRILLED SOFT-SHELL CRAB *Tacos* with HEIRLOOM TOMATO PICO DE GALLO

YIELD: 16 TACOS

Soft-shell crabs are found in the Gulf of Mexico and from Veracruz all the way to Louisiana. Every spring, when the season arrives in New York, you'll see these tacos at Dos Caminos until the last crab is pulled out of the water in September. The smoky char flavor of the grill, combined with the sweetness of the crab and the tart taste of the Pico de Gallo, is a flavor combo I look forward to each year. If the crabs are quite large, cut them in half and use 8 for 16 tacos.

16 small soft-shell crabs, cleaned
 (see the sidebar)

6 heirloom cherry tomatoes,
 cut into ½-inch dice

2 avocados, preferably Hass variety,
 peeled, seeded, and cut into ½-inch dice

1 red onion, thinly sliced

Leaves from 1 bunch cilantro,
 cut into chiffonade

1–2 *serrano* chiles, finely sliced

Juice of 2 limes, plus 2 limes
 cut into eighths, for garnish

¼ cup extra-virgin olive oil,
 plus 1 tablespoon to brush the crabs

Salt and freshly ground black pepper

16 corn tortillas, warmed

1. Clean the soft-shell crabs, or ask your fish vendor to do it for you.

2. In a small bowl, combine the tomatoes, avocados, onion, cilantro, chiles, lime juice, and ¼ cup of olive oil. Season to taste with salt and freshly ground black pepper and set aside.

3. Heat your grill to medium or build a medium-hot charcoal fire.

4. Brush the crabs with olive oil and lightly season with salt and pepper. Warm the tortillas.

5. Grill the crabs until lightly charred on the outside and cooked through, about 2 minutes per side. Serve in the tortillas with Heirloom Tomato *Pico de Gallo* and lime wedges.

CLEANING SOFT-SHELL CRABS

When you're buying soft-shell crabs, I suggest you buy them when they're in season and only from a reputable seafood purveyor. Optimally, buy those that are frisky, and certainly avoid any with an off smell. Keep them cold and use them within a day.

To clean crabs, using a pair of sharp kitchen shears, cut off the head just beyond the mouth and eyes. Next, flip the crabs over and remove the central flap-like apron at the opposite end by grabbing and pulling it down, then cutting it off with a sharp knife. Finally, lift up one pointed outer edge of the top shell enough so you can reach in and remove the fibrous gills. Repeat on the other side. Rinse the crabs well and pat dry.

GRILLED HOT *and* SMOKY SHRIMP *Tacos*

YIELD: 8 TACOS

The smoky taste of hot-off-the-grill shrimp combined with crunchy cabbage and red onion, tangy queso fresco, *creamy avocado, and* chipotle *sour cream is a perfect marriage and so easy to make. This is truly the perfect summer supper.*

8 flour tortillas

1 cup sour cream

2 teaspoons pureed *chipotles en adobo*

1 red onion, very thinly sliced

1 small head green cabbage, cored and thinly shredded

1 ripe avocado, preferably Hass variety, peeled and cut into 16 thin slices

½ cup *queso fresco*, crumbled or grated

¼ cup olive oil

16 extra-large raw shrimp, peeled and deveined

Fine sea salt and freshly ground black pepper

3–4 limes, halved

1. Heat a grill until hot. Wrap the tortillas in aluminum foil and warm on the grill or in the oven.

2. Meanwhile, in a small bowl, stir the sour cream and *chipotle* puree together until blended. Make an assembly line with bowls of the red onion, cabbage, avocado, and *queso fresco*.

3. Brush the grill with a little oil.

4. Toss the shrimp in oil and grill for about 2 minutes on each side, turning once. Season to taste with salt and pepper. Remove to a plate and cut in half lengthwise.

5. To assemble, put a slice of avocado in each tortilla. Add a generous sprinkle of cabbage and onion, followed by two shrimp per taco, and a generous spoonful of *chipotle* sour cream. Top with *queso fresco* and a light squeeze of lime.

SHRIMP *Tacos with* CHILE LIME SEA SALT *and* GRILLED PINEAPPLE *Salsita*

YIELD: 8 TACOS

Shrimp simmered in hot sauce is another outstanding taco filling. The heat of the shrimp combines well with smoky-sweet Pineapple Salsita and a dash of Chile Lime Sea Salt. There are many unique salts from around the world available to chefs and home cooks. One of my favorites is flaky Maldon salt from England. Four generations of the same family have harvested it since 1882. Opposite are some of my favorite spiced salts.

Chile Lime Sea Salt *(recipe follows)*

1 cup Grilled Pineapple Salsita *(recipe follows)*

¾ cup Dos Caminos's House Hot Sauce (page 31)

16 extra-large (16–20 per pound) shrimp, peeled, deveined, and cut in half lengthwise

8 flour tortillas

8 slices freshly cut avocado, preferably Hass variety

GRILLED PINEAPPLE SALSITA

3 (½-inch-thick) slices peeled and cored fresh pineapple

Blended oil, as needed

1 medium pink grapefruit, peeled, pith removed, and segmented

½ small jicama, peeled and julienned (about 1 cup)

3 very thin slices red onion

½ *jalapeño* pepper, seeded and minced

1½ teaspoons honey

1½ teaspoons freshly squeezed lime juice

½ teaspoon grated lime zest

Fine sea salt

¼ cup loosely packed cilantro leaves

I. Make the Chile Lime Sea Salt, Grilled Pineapple Salsita, and Dos Caminos's House Hot Sauce.

2. In a very large non-reactive skillet, over medium-high heat, sauté the shrimp in the House Hot Sauce until pink and just cooked through, 3 to 4 minutes. Divide them evenly among the tortillas.

3. Spoon the Grilled Pineapple Salsita over the shrimp. Top each with a slice of avocado, sprinkle with Chile Lime Sea Salt, and serve. Pass extra salsa at the table.

Grilled Pineapple Salsita

YIELD: 2 CUPS

This salsa is brimming with color, taste, and texture. Use on chicken, fish, or vegetarian tacos. To get the right amount of charred-sweet flavor from the pineapple, don't cut the pineapple slices too thin or they will fall apart; too thick and the pineapple won't develop the desired consistency and flavor.

Heat a grill until medium-hot. Using a pastry brush, lightly brush the pineapple with oil and grill until lightly browned with grill marks, about 2 minutes per side, and turn. Check often to see that the pineapple doesn't burn. Remove and let cool. Julienne the pineapple and combine it with the grapefruit, jicama, onion, *jalapeño,* honey, lime juice and zest, and salt to taste. Toss to blend. Reserve. Before serving, add the whole cilantro leaves and toss.

CHILE LIME SEA SALT

Finely grated zest of 8 limes

¼ cup crushed dried *chiles de árbol*

¼ cup coarse sea salt

2 tablespoons coriander seeds

ORANGE SEA SALT

2 large oranges

½ cup Maldon or other flaky salt

SMOKED CHILE SALT

½ cup smoked salt, available at gourmet stores and online

¾ teaspoon sweet *Pimentón de la Vera*

½ teaspoon hot paprika

Chile Lime Sea Salt

In a *molcajete* or using a mortar and pestle, mash the lime zest, dried chiles, sea salt, and coriander together until combined. Preheat the oven to 250 degrees, spread the salt on a flat pan, and roast until dry, about 15 minutes, turning occasionally.

Orange Sea Salt

1. Wash the oranges under cold running water and wipe dry. Let them sit at room temperature for 20 minutes.

2. Spread out the salt on a work surface. Working with one orange at a time, roll the orange over the salt with your palm. The coarse salt will become coated with the essential orange oils just below the skin of the orange.

3. Using a Microplane or a very fine zester, remove the zest from the oranges.

4. In a molcajete, crush the salt with the orange zest to a finer but still textured finish.

Smoked Chile Salt

In a small container with a lid, combine the salt, *Pimentón de la Vera,* and hot paprika. Seal and shake vigorously for several seconds until the chile powder is evenly distributed in the salt. You should not see large specks of red. Smoked Chile Salt will keep indefinitely.

SURF-and-TURF *Tacos* TAMPIQUEÑA-STYLE with *Pasilla de Oaxaca* TOMATILLO SALSA

YIELD: 16 TACOS

This dish looks like it has a lot of ingredients, but the steps are easy and the payoff is outstanding. Tampiqueña-*style refers to a steak dish named by Jose Luis Loredo,* a tampiqueño *waiter who went to Mexico City in 1939 to open the Tampico Club.* Carne asada á la tampiqueña *was his signature dish.*

½ cup blended oil

½ cup lime juice

2 tablespoons Worcestershire sauce

1 tablespoon rice vinegar

1 tablespoon dried oregano, preferably Mexican

1 teaspoon ancho chile powder

1 teaspoon garlic powder

1½ pounds skirt steak

½ recipe Guacamole (page 44)

3 strips smoky bacon, cooked and crumbled

Tomatillo *Pasilla de Oaxaca* Salsa (page 36)

½ cup Sriracha Lime Aioli *(recipe follows)*

Rock Shrimp *(recipe follows)*

2 radishes, thinly-sliced

1. To make the marinade: In a large, resealable plastic bag, combine the oil, lime juice, Worcestershire sauce, vinegar, oregano, chile powder, and garlic powder. Add the steak, turn to cover evenly, seal, and set aside to marinate.

2. Meanwhile, make the Guacamole and combine it with the bacon. Prepare the Tomatillo *Pasilla de Oaxaca* Salsa and Sriracha Lime Aioli (below).

3. Heat a grill or large heavy skillet over high heat until hot. Remove the steak from the marinade and cut it across the grain into thin slices. Grill the slices for 1½ minutes per side. Cut into medium dice, toss with the *Pasilla de Oaxaca* Tomatillo Salsa, and keep warm over low heat as you prepare the Rock Shrimp.

4. To assemble the tacos, spoon a teaspoon of Bacon Guacamole onto each tortilla. Divide the meat followed by the shrimp equally in the tacos and finish with a generous drizzle of Sriracha Lime Aioli. Garnish with thinly-sliced radishes.

1 cup mayonnaise, not light variety

1 tablespoon freshly squeezed lime juice

1 tablespoon Sriracha chile sauce

½ tablespoon Old Bay seasoning

½ teaspoon finely grated lime zest

⅛ teaspoon fine sea salt

ROCK SHRIMP

2 tablespoons unsalted butter

1½ pounds rock shrimp, cleaned

1 small *guajillo* chile, seeded and very thinly sliced

Juice of 1 lime

Fine sea salt and freshly ground black pepper

16 flour tortillas

Sriracha Lime Aioli

In a small bowl, whisk together the mayonnaise, lime juice, Sriracha, Old Bay seasoning, lime zest, and salt to taste.

Rock Shrimp

In a large skillet, melt the butter over medium-high heat. Add the shrimp and sauté until they just start to turn pink. Stir in the chile, add the lime juice, and cook for 1 minute more. Season to taste with salt and pepper.

LOBSTER *Tacos* PUERTO *Nuevo Style*

YIELD: 16 TACOS

In Puerto Nuevo, a seaside resort in Baja, on the Pacific coast of Mexico, spiny lobsters are abundant and delicious. Reputedly over a million of the spiny crustaceans are served each year. Eating tacos made with them is like a trip back to Old Baja in my college days for me. Please (if possible) don't steam them! Spiny lobsters are best when grilled or, as in the classic style of Puerto Nuevo, deep-fried in lard.

The traditional way to eat them is to place some refried beans in the center of the tortilla, top with a lobster tail, then drizzle with melted butter (margarine in the old days!), salsas, and lime juice. Wash them down with ice-cold soda or beer.

2 cups My Refried Beans (page 228)

1 cup Roasted Tomato *Chile de Árbol* Salsa (page 34)

Pico de Gallo (page 39)

2 pounds lard

8 (1½-pound) lobsters

½ pound (2 sticks) unsalted butter

8 (12-inch) flour tortillas, preferably handmade

2 limes, cut into eighths

1. Prepare My Refried Beans using pinto beans, the Roasted Tomato *Chile de Árbol* Salsa, and *Pico de Gallo*. Set aside.

2. In a large, deep, heavy casserole, melt the lard over medium heat until it measures 375 degrees on an instant-read thermometer.

3. With a heavy, sharp knife, split the lobsters in half lengthwise. Remove the green vein and flesh from the head and discard. Rinse and pat dry thoroughly. Carefully place the lobster halves into the hot lard, a couple at a time, and cook for about 5 minutes, until the tails are curled and red.

4. Meanwhile, melt the butter and heat the Refried Beans and tortillas.

5. Using tongs, remove the lobsters from the oil and drain well on paper towels. Remove the meat from the shells and pile in the center of a platter.

6. Rinse the shells. Fill them with My Refried Beans, *Pico de Gallo*, Roasted Tomato *Chile de Árbol* Salsa, and limes, arranging around the lobster tails. Serve with warm melted butter and flour tortillas on the side.

FISH *and* SEAFOOD *Tacos*

SCALLOP and CHORIZO *Tacos*

YIELD: 16 TACOS

Scallops and pork, pork and scallops: one of my favorite flavor combinations. Once the garlic is sliced (if you have a mandoline or a thin slicing blade on your food processor, it's much easier), the dish takes very little work to make. Although a lot of garlic is used, it's added at three different times during the preparation and the taste is mild. Poblano chiles, crema, and Cotija cheese complement it.

1 pound tomatoes, cored and
    coarsely chopped

4 small cloves garlic,
    plus ½ cup sliced garlic

2 small white onions, coarsely chopped

2 small *poblano* chiles, seeds and
    membranes removed, coarsely chopped

½ cup firmly packed, coarsely chopped
    flat-leaf parsley, plus additional chopped
    parsley for garnish

¾ cup extra-virgin olive oil

½ pound fresh Mexican chorizo,
    casings removed

1 pound bay scallops, blotted dry

Fine sea salt

2 large bay leaves, broken into pieces

1 teaspoon sugar

Freshly ground black pepper

16 corn tortillas

Crema, Greek yogurt, or crème fraîche,
    for garnish

¾ cup julienned radishes, for garnish

1 cup crumbled *Cotija* cheese, for garnish

1. In the jar of an electric blender, combine the tomatoes, the 4 whole cloves garlic, the onions, the *poblano* chiles, and ½ cup parsley. Blend for a few seconds to make a textured puree. Set aside.

2. In a large skillet, heat the oil over medium heat. Add half of the sliced garlic and fry until golden brown, watching that it doesn't burn. Remove with a slotted spoon and discard.

3. Add the chorizo to the skillet, turn the heat to high, and sauté for 4 minutes. Turn the heat down to medium-high and continue cooking until the chorizo is golden brown, 6 to 7 minutes, breaking up the pieces with a wooden spatula.

4. Stir the remaining garlic into the pan with the chorizo. Add the scallops, sprinkle with salt, and quickly sauté, stirring occasionally, for 2 minutes.

5. Add the tomato puree, bay leaves, sugar, and pepper to taste. Cook briefly to reduce the sauce, about 3 minutes. The scallops should be tender.

6. Warm the tortillas on a griddle or in the oven and fill each with the scallop mixture. Drizzle each with *crema*, top with a sprinkle of julienned radishes, and sprinkle with *Cotija* cheese and the remaining parsley.

OCTOPUS Ceviche Tacos

YIELD: 16 TACOS

When I need a getaway, I often head to Isla Mujeres, a quiet island off of Cancún, where I eat fresh pulpo ceviche *every day with my toes in the sand. Grilled octopus will always bring me back to Isla's waterfront and the fresh taste of clean ocean spray. Here the octopus is first blanched, then lightly grilled. It's then combined with a colorful and refreshing salad, and topped with smoky* Pasilla de Oaxaca *Chile Salsa.*

Pasilla de Oaxaca Chile Salsa *(recipe follows)*

1 small red onion, cut lengthwise into thin strips

1–2 *serrano* chiles, seeded and chopped

½ cup cherry tomatoes, quartered

½ cup pitted Kalamata olives, quartered

½ cup lima beans, cooked until tender

¼ cup chopped cilantro leaves

3 small scallions, including light green parts

4–5 tablespoons extra-virgin olive oil

2 tablespoons freshly squeezed lemon juice

Kosher salt and freshly ground black pepper

1 (2- to 3-pound) octopus

1 cup rice vinegar

1 tablespoon freshly squeezed lime juice

2 tablespoons lemon oil or olive oil

16 tortillas, warmed

Leaves from 1 small head mâche lettuce

PASILLA DE OAXACA CHILE SALSA

5 *pasilla de Oaxaca* chiles, stemmed, seeded, toasted, and rehydrated

1 clove garlic

¾ cup rice vinegar

1¼ cups blended oil

Fine sea salt

1. Prepare the *Pasilla de Oaxaca* Chile Salsa.

2. In a bowl, combine the onion, *serranos,* tomatoes, olives, lima beans, cilantro, and scallions. Drizzle on about 3 tablespoons of the olive oil and the lemon juice, season to taste with salt and pepper, and toss. Add more oil, as needed.

3. In a medium-sized non-reactive pot, combine the octopus with enough water to cover. Add the vinegar and a tablespoon of salt and bring to a boil over high heat. Reduce the heat so the liquid is gently simmering, cover, and blanch the octopus for 5 minutes. Remove and cool. Using a sharp knife, cut off the tentacles.

4. Heat a gas or charcoal grill or heavy grill pan until medium-hot.

5. Toss the tentacles with a little of the remaining oil and grill until brown marks form on both sides, turning once. Remove, cool, and cut into ¼-inch dice. Toss with the lime juice and lemon oil and season with salt and pepper.

6. Divide the octopus among the tortillas, spoon on the salad, drizzle with *Pasilla de Oaxaca* Chile Salsa, and garnish with a few mâche leaves.

Pasilla de Oaxaca Chile Salsa

In the jar of an electric blender, combine the chiles with the garlic and rice vinegar and puree until smooth. With the motor running, slowly drizzle in the oil. Season to taste with salt.

POULTRY
Tacos

WOOD-CHARCOAL-GRILLED CHICKEN *Tacos*

YIELD: 16 TACOS

In Mexico, grilling is done al carbon, *over wood charcoal. While the "kings" of the grill show their skills, the women make the salsas, and the little girls prepare tortillas for a backyard fiesta. These zesty, marinated chicken tacos are very simple to make.*

⅔ cup freshly squeezed orange juice

⅓ cup freshly squeezed lime juice

¼ cup *achiote* paste

8 cloves garlic

3 *jalapeños*

2 tablespoons Maggi sauce

1 tablespoon whole black peppercorns

1 tablespoon kosher salt

1 bunch cilantro

2 pounds chicken legs and thighs

Pico de Gallo (page 39)

16 corn tortillas

1 cup grated *Cotija* cheese, for garnish

1 cup *crema*, Greek yogurt,
  or crème fraîche, for garnish

½ cup cilantro leaves, for garnish

1. For the marinade: In the jar of an electric blender, combine the orange juice, lime juice, *achiote* paste, garlic, *jalapeños,* Maggi sauce, peppercorns, salt, and cilantro; puree until smooth. Rub the marinade all over the chicken, put the pieces in a large, flat, glass baking dish, cover, and refrigerate for at least 1 hour or preferably overnight.

2. Heat the oven to 350 degrees.

3. Transfer the chicken to a roasting pan and roast until the meat easily pulls away from the bone, about 45 minutes. Remove the pan from the oven and let the chicken cool. When cool, remove and discard the skin and bones and shred the meat into large pieces. Reserve the cooking liquid. Refrigerate the chicken if you're not using it right away.

4. While the chicken cools, prepare the *Pico de Gallo*.

5. Reheat the chicken in the cooking juices in a warm oven or over low heat on top of the stove. Toast each tortilla in a nonstick pan over medium heat for about 30 seconds on each side. Wrap in a towel to keep warm.

6. Divide the chicken among the tortillas, topping with *Pico de Gallo, Cotija* cheese, *crema,* and chopped cilantro.

CHICKEN CHORIZO and POTATO Tacos

YIELD: 12 TACOS

*Robust, spicy chorizo has long been a staple in traditional Mexican recipes.
Recently, the sausages typically made with pork are also being made with ground chicken and other
meats. With plenty of seasonings, the taste of the chicken version is similar and quite satisfying.
Spanish chorizo is already cured when you buy it; the Mexican version is sold raw
and removed from the casings before cooking.*

1 pound unpeeled red potatoes,
  cut into ½-inch dice

Fine sea salt

2 teaspoons blended oil

12 ounces Mexican chicken chorizo
  sausage, casing removed
  (about 1½ cups)

½ cup finely chopped white onions

3 tomatillos, husked, washed,
  and coarsely chopped

2 *serrano* chiles, stemmed and coarsely
  chopped

1 large clove garlic, coarsely chopped

12 corn tortillas, warmed

1 large avocado, halved, seeded, peeled,
  and sliced

1. In a large saucepan, bring 1 to 2 quarts of water to a boil. Add the potatoes and 2 teaspoons of salt. Cover and cook until just tender, 10 to 12 minutes. Drain.

2. Heat a large skillet over medium heat. Add the oil, sausage, and onion and sauté until the sausage is cooked through and the onions are tender, about 10 minutes, breaking up the sausage meat with a wooden spatula and stirring occasionally. Drain and discard all but 1 to 2 tablespoons of the excess fat in the pan.

3. Meanwhile, prepare the tomatillo salsa: Combine the tomatillos, *serrano* chiles, and garlic in the jar of an electric blender and puree until smooth. Season to taste with salt and set aside.

4. Add the potatoes to the skillet and cook until the potatoes begin to brown, about 6 minutes, tossing occasionally. Keep warm. Spoon into the tortillas, garnish with avocado slices and tomatillo salsa, and serve.

CHICKEN MEATBALL
Tacos

YIELD: 14 TACOS

Meatballs or albondigas *in broth are a Mexican tradition.*
For this homey version, I first make chicken soup and then shred the cooked meat for the meatballs.
It's simple and satisfying. Serve in tortillas with the broth on the side,
or reserve the broth for another use.

6 cloves garlic

1 white onion, coarsely chopped

1 *poblano* pepper, stemmed,
    seeded, and coarsely chopped

1 tablespoon *achiote* paste

3 tablespoons blended oil

2 cups Maseca-brand *masa harina*

1-plus teaspoons fine sea salt

2 cups My Chicken Broth, strained
    (recipe follows)

½ cup cilantro leaves and stems,
    finely chopped, plus additional leaves
    for garnish

¼ cup mint leaves, finely chopped,
    plus additional leaves for garnish

2 tablespoons freshly squeezed
    orange juice

1 tablespoon freshly squeezed lime juice

14 corn tortillas

1. Make the meatballs: In a food processor, combine the garlic, onion, and *poblano;* pulse until the mixture is a fine paste.

2. In a large skillet, heat the oil over medium heat. Add the onion mixture and *achiote* paste and cook for about 5 minutes, stirring occasionally. Transfer to a large bowl, add the Maseca and 1 teaspoon of salt, and mix.

3. Add 2 cups of the strained broth, the cilantro, mint, orange juice, and the shredded chicken. Stir until thoroughly combined.

4. Bring the broth to a simmer over medium-low heat. Shape the dough into a 1½-inch ball and add to the simmering broth. Taste and add salt to the *masa,* if needed. Shape the remaining dough into meatballs and cook until they float to the surface, 5 to 7 minutes. Using a slotted spoon, remove the meatballs to warm corn tortillas and serve hot, garnished with cilantro and mint leaves.

1 large chicken, cut into 8 pieces

10 cloves garlic, smashed

1 white onion, peeled and quartered

1 *poblano* pepper, stemmed,
    seeded, and quartered

2 limes, cut in half

1 orange, cut in half

½ bunch cilantro, leaves and stems

¼ cup packed mint leaves

4 allspice berries

1 (4-inch) piece of cinnamon,
    preferably Mexican *canela*

1 tablespoon kosher salt

2 teaspoons whole black peppercorns

My Chicken Broth

1. In a large soup pot, combine 3 quarts of water with the chicken, garlic, onion, *poblano,* limes, orange, cilantro, and mint. Add the allspice, cinnamon, salt, and peppercorns and bring to a boil over high heat, skimming the surface of foam.

2. Reduce the heat to medium-low and gently simmer until the chicken is cooked through, about 18 minutes, skimming the surface occasionally.

3. With a slotted spoon, transfer the chicken to a large bowl. When it's cool enough to handle, remove the chicken skin and bones and discard. Finely shred the chicken. Strain the broth back into the soup pot. Reserve the chicken meat for another use, such as chicken tacos.

CHICKEN CARNITAS
Tacos

YIELD: 16 TACOS

In this version of carnitas (which translates as "little meats"), dark meat chicken, instead of the more traditional pork, is simmered in condensed milk, Coca-Cola, and orange juice. It's a classic method of cooking in Mexico that imparts a rich caramel-creamy taste. Save your chicken fat for this dish. Although this looks like a lot of fat, fear not: Most of it stays in the pan once the chicken is tender. Like meat cooked on the bone, chicken is generally juicier and has more flavor this way.

3-plus pounds chicken fat or vegetable shortening

3 pounds bone-in chicken legs and thighs

1 (14-ounce) can sweetened condensed milk

1 (12-ounce) can Coca-Cola

¾ cup freshly squeezed orange juice

10 whole black peppercorns

5 bay leaves

1 tablespoon kosher salt

16 tortillas

1. In a large, deep, heavy pot, melt the lard over medium heat.

2. Add the chicken, condensed milk, Coca-Cola, orange juice, peppercorns, bay leaves, and salt. Cook over medium heat until the chicken is very tender and can be easily shredded, 1 to 1½ hours, adding more lard if needed to cover the chicken completely.

3. Remove the pan from the heat. With a slotted spoon, lift the chicken from the braising liquid, discard the skin and bones, shred the meat, and spoon onto tortillas. Add the toppings of your choice.

CHICKEN *Picadillo Tacos*

YIELD: 12 TACOS

Brimming with savory and sweet flavors and a variety of textures,
this is a lighter version of an old favorite taco usually made with beef or pork.
The filling needs little adornment except perhaps some crema, *and your favorite salsa.*

1 tablespoon blended oil

3 cloves garlic, finely chopped

1 white onion, cut into fine dice

1 *poblano* pepper, seeds and membranes removed, cut into fine dice

1 cup tomato paste

¼ cup ground *ancho* chile powder

2 pounds ground chicken

¼ cup dry sherry

2 cups canned tomato sauce

1 red potato, peeled, cut into ¼-inch dice, and fried until crisp

1 *habañero* chile, minced

½ cup sliced almonds, lightly toasted

½ cup diced dried apricots

½ cup sliced green olives

¼ cup golden raisins

1 tablespoon Valentina or other brand hot sauce

Fine sea salt and freshly ground black pepper

12 corn tortillas, warmed

Crema, for garnish *(optional)*

Chopped cilantro, for garnish *(optional)*

1. In a heavy saucepan, combine the oil, garlic, onion, and pepper; cover and sweat over medium-low heat until soft, 3 to 5 minutes, stirring occasionally. Stir in the tomato paste and chile powder, then add the chicken and cook until browned, breaking the pieces apart with a wooden spatula.

2. Pour in the sherry, bring to a boil over high heat, and stir up any browned cooking bits. Stir in the tomato sauce, potato, *habañero,* almonds, apricots, olives, raisins, Valentina hot sauce, and salt and pepper to taste. Return the mixture to a simmer.

3. Divide the filling among the tortillas. If desired, drizzle with *crema* and cilantro before serving.

CHICKEN TINGA
Tacos

YIELD: 14 TACOS

Chicken Tinga, shredded braised chicken in tomato chipotle sauce, is Puebla's answer to soul food. Even before you take a bite, the spicy-smoky aroma from the pan will captivate you. If you make your own chicken stock, reserve the cooking liquid from this recipe to use as the base of it.

Roasted Tomato Salsita *(recipe follows)*

1 (3- to 3½-pound) whole chicken

1 stalk celery, coarsely chopped

1 carrot, coarsely chopped

1 white onion, coarsely chopped

½ cup kosher salt

3 sprigs fresh thyme

1 bay leaf

1 teaspoon whole black peppercorns

14 corn tortillas, warmed

1 cup crumbled *Cotija* cheese, for garnish

1 cup thinly sliced scallions, for garnish

ROASTED TOMATO SALSITA

4 Roma tomatoes, quartered lengthwise

1 tablespoon blended oil

1 large white onion, thinly sliced

1–2 *chipotles en adobo*, pureed

2 teaspoons chopped *piloncillo*,
    Sugar in the Raw, or turbinado sugar

1–2 teaspoons rice or apple cider vinegar

Fine sea salt

1. Prepare the Roasted Tomato Salsita.

2. When the salsita is close to being finished, in a large pot, combine the chicken, celery, carrot, onion, salt, thyme, bay leaf, and peppercorns. Add cold water to cover completely, cover the pot, and bring it to a boil over high heat. Reduce the heat and simmer until the chicken reaches an internal temperature of 165 degrees on an instant-read thermometer, about 30 minutes.

3. Remove the chicken from the liquid and cool, reserving the liquid. Pull the meat from the carcass, shred it into large pieces, and mix with sauce, thinning the sauce with a little of the cooking liquid. Spoon the chicken onto the tortillas and garnish with *Cotija* cheese and scallions.

Roasted Tomato Salsita

1. Preheat the oven to 250 degrees.

2. Toss the tomatoes with a little oil and roast in a flat pan in the oven until dry, 2 to 3 hours, turning occasionally. In a large deep skillet, heat the remaining oil over medium-high heat. Add the onion and sauté until deep golden brown, turning often. Add the tomatoes.

3. While the tomatoes are roasting, in a small saucepan, combine ¼ cup of water with the *chipotles, piloncillo,* and vinegar; simmer for 15 minutes. Scrape this into the skillet with the tomatoes and onions, mix well, and season to taste with salt.

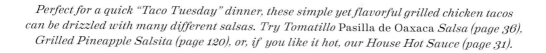

Easy GRILLED LIME CHICKEN Tacos

YIELD: 8 TACOS

Perfect for a quick "Taco Tuesday" dinner, these simple yet flavorful grilled chicken tacos can be drizzled with many different salsas. Try Tomatillo Pasilla de Oaxaca *Salsa (page 36), Grilled Pineapple Salsita (page 120), or, if you like it hot, our House Hot Sauce (page 31).*

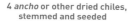

4 *ancho* or other dried chiles, stemmed and seeded

2–3 cloves garlic, crushed or minced

3 tablespoons freshly squeezed lime juice

1 *jalapeño*

4 limes, cut into ¼-inch slices

Fine sea salt

5 (5- to 6-ounce) boneless, skinless chicken breasts

Tomatillo *Pasilla de Oaxaca* Salsa (page 36)

8 corn tortillas, warmed

1. Rehydrate the chiles in hot water, drain, and transfer to the jar of an electric blender. Reserve the soaking liquid in case it is needed while pureeing the chiles. Add the garlic, lime juice, and *jalapeño* to the jar and puree until smooth. Scrape into a bowl and fold the lime slices into the chile mixture along with ½ teaspoon of the salt. Coat the chicken with the mixture, cover, and refrigerate for up to 8 hours.

2. Prepare the Tomatillo *Pasilla de Oaxaca* Salsa or your favorite salsa. Heat a grill or grill pan until hot.

3. Remove the chicken from the marinade and season with salt. Lay the pieces on the grill and cook until just cooked through, 5 to 6 minutes per side, turning once. Remove, slice across the grain, and serve with warm corn tortillas and salsa.

FRIED CHICKEN
Tacos

YIELD: 16 TACOS

Mexicans feel it's bad to waste any part of an animal that's edible. On my most recent trip to Baja, California, a culinary melting pot of Mexican American and even Chinese influences, I discovered Kentucky Fried Buches, a Tijuana institution that has been serving fried chicken necks since 1963. They deep-fry the necks to where they are so crisp-tender you can actually eat the bones, and then serve them with spicy salsa and warm corn tortillas. I use thighs here, but feel free to experiment with the necks for a real Tijuana specialty. Of course, an ice-cold Tecate is a must!

In this recipe, southern-grown pecans seem to have a natural affinity for another southern staple: fried chicken. I learned about this salsa from Rick Bayless, the great Mexican chef from Chicago, while we were both in Baja.

Juice of 2 limes

Fine sea salt

8 large boneless chicken thighs with skin on

Salsa *Macha* (recipe follows)

¼ cup all-purpose flour

¼ cup Maseca-brand *masa* for tortillas

½ teaspoon hot *Pimentón de la Vera*

¼ teaspoon *chile de árbol* powder

Blended oil for frying

16 corn tortillas, warm

SALSA *MACHA*

2 cups olive oil

⅓ cup pecan pieces

1 tablespoon sesame seeds

4 cloves garlic, peeled and halved

15 dried *chiles de árbol*, stemmed and seeded (about 1 cup)

1 tablespoon apple cider vinegar

1 teaspoon fine sea salt

Generous ½ teaspoon dried oregano, preferably Mexican

1. In a large bowl or casserole, whisk together the lime juice and 1 teaspoon of salt until blended. Add the thighs and turn to coat thoroughly. Cover and marinate in the refrigerator for 2 hours or up to overnight.

2. Prepare the Salsa *Macha*.

3. Remove the chicken thighs and pat dry with paper towels.

4. In a small bowl, combine the flour, *Maseca, Pimentón, chile de árbol* powder, and 1 teaspoon of salt.

5. In a large, deep frying pan, heat 1 inch of oil over medium-high heat until hot and shimmering. Dredge the chicken pieces in the seasoned flour, patting to remove the excess. Slowly add the pieces to the oil, taking care not to crowd, and fry until the pieces are golden brown, are very crisp, and measure about 170 degrees on an instant-read thermometer, about 4 minutes per side. Using tongs, remove to paper towels to drain. Cut the chicken into thin strips and serve with Salsa *Macha* and tortillas.

Salsa *Macha*

In a large saucepan, combine the oil, pecans, sesame seeds, and garlic. Cook over medium-high heat until the garlic and sesame seeds are golden, about 5 minutes. Remove from the heat and stir in the chiles. Let cool 5 minutes. In a small bowl, mix the vinegar with the salt until the salt dissolves, then add it to the pan along with the oregano. Cool to room temperature, pour it into the jar of an electric blender or food processor along with 3 to 4 tablespoons of the oil, and pulse until everything is chopped into small pieces. Run the processor for a few more seconds until everything is finely chopped.

MARINATED CHICKEN SUPREMO *Tacos* *with Chicharonnes*

YIELD: 16 TACOS

My inspiration for these spicy-sweet marinated chicken thighs was the addictive, crispy-skinned chicken served at the wildly popular El Pollo Supremo, near my mom's house in Scottsdale, Arizona.

2¼ pounds large chicken thighs with skin and bones

Juice of 2 lemons

Juice of 2 oranges

1 cup Valentina or other hot sauce

¼ cup extra-virgin olive oil

¼ cup rice vinegar

1½ tablespoons Maggi sauce

1½ tablespoons sugar

1½ tablespoons crushed garlic

2 teaspoons Dos Caminos's House Hot Sauce (page 31)

2 cups My Refried Beans (page 228)

Chile de Árbol Salsa (recipe follows)

Chicharonnes (recipe follows)

12 scallions, including most of the green parts, trimmed

16 corn tortillas, warmed

¾ cup *queso fresco*, crumbled, for garnish

1. Remove the skin from the chicken and reserve for the *chicharonnes*. In a large bowl, whisk together the lemon and orange juices, Valentina sauce, oil, vinegar, Maggi, sugar, garlic, and House Hot Sauce. Pour the mixture into a very large resealable plastic bag, add the chicken, turn to coat evenly, and marinate in the refrigerator for 24 hours, turning a couple of times.

2. Meanwhile, prepare My Refried Beans, *Chile de Árbol* Salsa, and *chicharonnes*.

3. Before grilling the chicken, reheat My Refried Beans, if needed. Heat a grill or heavy grill pan to hot. Remove the chicken from the marinade and lay the pieces on the grill, taking care not to crowd them. Cook until an instant-read thermometer reads 165 degrees or the juices run clear when the meat is pricked deeply near the bone, turning once. Grill the scallions at the same time until they are nicely charred. Remove and slice on the bias into 1-inch pieces.

4. Remove the chicken and, when it's cool enough to handle, pull the meat from the bones. Cut it into bite-sized pieces and keep warm.

5. Spoon a tablespoon of My Refried Beans onto each tortilla. Divide the chicken among the tortillas, lightly drizzle on *Chile de Árbol* Salsa, sprinkle with scallions and *chicharonnes,* and serve.

10 *chiles de árbol*, stemmed and seeded

1 allspice berry

1 whole clove

1 large clove garlic, coarsely chopped

1 tablespoon pumpkin seeds, or *pepitas*, toasted

½ tablespoon sesame seeds, toasted

¼ teaspoon dried oregano, preferably Mexican

½ teaspoon fine sea salt

¼ teaspoon cumin seeds, toasted

¼ cup apple cider vinegar

CHICHARONNES

¼ cup freshly squeezed lime juice

¼ cup dark rum

¼ cup soy sauce

1 tablespoon sugar

Skin from chicken thighs (above)

½ cup all-purpose flour

½ teaspoon smoked paprika, such as *Pimentón de la Vera*

½ teaspoon fine sea salt

2 tablespoons blended oil for frying

Chile de Árbol Salsa

In the jar of an electric blender, combine the chiles, allspice, clove, garlic, pumpkin seeds, sesame seeds, oregano, salt, and cumin seeds. With the motor running, slowly pour in the vinegar and puree until very smooth. Taste to adjust the salt, if necessary. Scrape into a bowl and cover.

Chicharonnes

1. Prepare the marinade: In a bowl, stir the lime juice, rum, soy sauce, and sugar together until the sugar has dissolved. Add the chicken skin and marinate for 30 minutes at room temperature.

2. In a bowl, whisk together the flour, paprika, and salt. Remove the pieces from the marinade and pat dry with paper towels. Dredge in the flour mixture and transfer to a plate.

3. In a large heavy skillet, heat the oil over medium-high heat until hot and shimmering. Add the chicken skin and fry until deep golden brown and cooked through, turning to cook evenly. Remove to paper towels to drain and crumble into bite-sized pieces for garnish.

SMOKED CHICKEN THIGH *Tacos with* WATERMELON *Pico de Gallo*

YIELD: 16 TACOS

Applewood chips impart a fruity-smoky taste to these chicken thighs marinated in a spicy-sweet mixture before grilling. Watermelon Pico de Gallo *alongside makes a delightfully refreshing partner. The two sugars have different flavors: The dark brown sugar is more caramelized while Sugar in the Raw is like Mexican cone sugar, called* piloncillo.

½ cup firmly packed dark brown sugar

¼ cup Sugar in the Raw or turbinado sugar

¼ cup kosher salt

2 tablespoons paprika

½ tablespoon freshly ground black pepper

½ tablespoon white pepper

½ tablespoon onion powder

½ tablespoon garlic powder

½ teaspoon ground cumin

½ teaspoon ground celery seed

½ teaspoon *ancho* chile powder

¼ teaspoon *chile de árbol* powder

1 cup apple juice

2½ pounds bone-in chicken thighs

Watermelon *Pico de Gallo* (page 43)

Applewood chips, soaked in water overnight, for the smoker

2 ripe avocados, preferably Hass variety

16 corn tortillas, warmed

Cotija cheese, crumbled

1. In a large bowl, mix together the brown sugar, Sugar in the Raw, salt, paprika, black pepper, white pepper, onion powder, garlic powder, cumin, celery seed, and *ancho* and *árbol* chile powders. Stir in the apple juice, add the chicken thighs, and turn until well coated. Marinate in the refrigerator for at least 2 hours or overnight.

2. Prepare the Watermelon *Pico de Gallo*.

3. Add the applewood chips to a smoker and heat to 220 degrees.

4. Lay the thighs on racks on sheet trays in the smoker and smoke until they reach an internal temperature of 165 degrees when measured with an instant-read thermometer inserted deep in the flesh, 45 minutes to 1 hour.

5. Remove the chicken thighs, then cool until you can shred the meat with your hands. Slice the avocados.

6. Divide the chicken among the tortillas, spoon on some Watermelon *Pico de Gallo,* add the avocados and *Cotija* cheese, and serve the remaining salsa at the table.

CHOPPED CHICKEN LIVER *Tacos*

YIELD: 16 TACOS

I adore chicken livers, especially when chopped into a coarse pâté-like consistency.
Mexico City has one of the largest Jewish populations in the world, and I serve this dish
for their holidays. Soaking livers in milk helps remove any bitterness.
Serve them with my Matzo Tortillas (below); because corn tortillas are unleavened,
they may be eaten during Passover.

Matzo Tortillas *(recipe follows)*, heated

2 pounds chicken livers

1 quart whole milk, for soaking

4 ounces (1 cube or ½ stick)
  unsalted butter

6 cloves garlic, minced

4 canned anchovy fillets, chopped

2 medium white onions, diced

¼ cup white wine

½ cup chicken stock

Zest of 1 orange

¼ cup sherry vinegar

¼ cup honey

¼ cup mayonnaise, not light variety

2 tablespoons chopped *chipotles en adobo*

6 large eggs, hard-cooked and chopped,
  2 reserved for garnish

Fine sea salt and freshly ground
  black pepper

GARNISHES

1 cup minced red onion

1 cup chopped cilantro

¾ cup chopped flat-leaf parsley

¾ cup sliced pickled *jalapeños*

1. Prepare the Matzo Tortillas. Meanwhile, in a bowl, soak the chicken livers in milk for an hour. Drain and blot dry.

2. In a large skillet, heat the butter over medium heat. Add the garlic, anchovies, and onions and sauté until the onions are soft but not browned, about 3 minutes, mashing the anchovies with a fork.

3. Turn the heat up to medium-high, add the livers, and sauté until golden brown, about 4 minutes. Pour in the wine and cook until most of the liquid evaporates. Stir in the stock and simmer until the livers are cooked through and the liquid has reduced by half, about 10 minutes, breaking the livers up with a fork or wooden spatula. Cool slightly.

4. Scrape the mixture into a food processor and pulse into a coarsely chopped puree. Mix in the orange zest, vinegar, honey, mayonnaise, *chipotles*, and four of the chopped eggs. Season with salt and pepper to taste.

5. Spoon the chopped liver into the Matzo Tortillas. Sprinkle with a generous amount of red onion, eggs, cilantro, parlsey, and *jalapeños* and serve.

MATZO TORTILLAS

1 cup matzo meal, ground to the consistency of flour

½ teaspoon fine sea salt

1 tablespoon blended oil, to grease the pan

Matzo Tortillas

YIELD: MAKES 16

1. In a bowl, combine the matzo meal, 1 cup of water, and salt. Mix by hand to the consistency of *masa*.

2. Preheat a cast-iron skillet or griddle to medium heat. Brush with oil.

3. Wet your hands and mold the dough into 16 small balls. Using a tortilla press, a rolling pin, two heavy books, or your hands, press each ball of dough flat into a 3-inch circle between two sheets of plastic wrap.

4. Put a tortilla in the preheated pan and cook for 1 to 2 minutes per side or until slightly browned. Turn, cook the second side for about 1 to 2 minutes, and transfer to a plate. Repeat the process with each ball of dough. Keep the tortillas covered with a towel to stay warm and moist until ready to serve.

POULTRY *Tacos*

DUCK *Carnitas* *Tacos*

YIELD: 16 TACOS

Here's another use for that magical Mexican marriage of Coca-Cola, condensed milk, and orange juice: It turns duck meat into a powerhouse taco filling. To make it even more interesting, the duck skin is crisped, chopped, and mixed with the succulent meat. Grilled Peach and Red Pepper Salsita (page 55) would be a perfect balance for the duck.

Grilled Peach and Red Pepper Salsita
  (page 55)

4-plus pounds duck fat or lard

6 pounds duck leg-thigh combinations

½ cup orange juice

½ cup Coca-Cola

¾ cup sweetened condensed milk

5 bay leaves

1 sprig fresh thyme

½ stick cinnamon, preferably
  Mexican *canela*

Zest of 1 orange

1 whole *chile de árbol*, stemmed

1 tablespoon whole peppercorns

Fine sea salt

16 corn tortillas, warmed

1. Prepare the Grilled Peach and Red Pepper Salsita.

2. Preheat the oven to 300 degrees.

3. In a large, deep pot, melt the lard. Add the duck, orange juice, Coca-Cola, condensed milk, bay leaves, thyme, cinnamon, orange zest, *chile de árbol,* peppercorns, and a couple teaspoons of salt, making sure the duck is completely submerged in the liquid. Add more, if needed. Bring to a simmer over medium heat.

4. Transfer the pot to the oven and cook until the duck is very tender when pricked with a fork, 2 to 3 hours. Remove from the oven.

5. Heat a large, heavy skillet over medium-high heat. Add the duck pieces and cook until the skin is crisp and brown on the outside. Taste to adjust the salt.

6. Remove the skin and chop it into small pieces. Remove the meat from the bones and tear into large pieces, being careful not to shred it too finely. Discard the bones.

7. Divide the duck among the tortillas, spoon on the salsa, and serve. Pass extra salsa at the table.

DUCK TACOS with PLUM
Pico de Gallo

YIELD: 16 TACOS

*For the most part, I stick to taco fillings that would or could be eaten in Mexico.
Sometimes, however, I go off that beaten path. These tacos are my homage to the awesome Peking duck
I was served at Li Qun, a ramshackle dump of a restaurant in a dodgy part of Beijing.
It's a word-of-mouth sensation that you find by following pictures of ducks posted along winding roads.
The adventure more than exceeded my expectations.*

1 (2½- to 3-pound) Pekin (Long Island) duck, excess fat removed

1 cup red wine

1 cup soy sauce

¼ cup hoisin sauce

1 tablespoon freshly squeezed lime juice

1 teaspoon Sichuan peppercorns

3 cloves garlic, smashed

1 (4-inch) stick cinnamon, preferably Mexican *canela*

1 *chile de árbol*, crumbled

1 (½-inch) piece fresh ginger, smashed

1 small white onion, coarsely chopped

Plum *Pico de Gallo* (recipe follows)

2 tablespoons blended oil

16 (6-inch) flour tortillas, warmed

Cilantro sprigs, for garnish

PLUM *PICO DE GALLO*

1 pound ripe plums, pitted and diced

½ cup finely chopped fresh cilantro

⅓ cup minced red onion

¼ cup finely chopped fresh mint leaves

1 small jalapeño, minced

1 tablespoon freshly squeezed lime juice

2 teaspoons sugar, or to taste

Fine sea salt

1. Wash and dry the duck. Tie the legs together with string, then tuck the wings under the body to secure them.

2. In a large bowl or casserole, combine the wine, soy, hoisin, lime juice, peppercorns, garlic, *canela, chile de árbol,* ginger, and onion. Add the duck and marinate in the refrigerator for 2 hours or up to overnight.

3. Position the oven rack in the middle of the oven and preheat to 375 degrees.

4. Transfer the duck to a roasting pan and reserve the marinade. Roast for 15 minutes. Meanwhile, pour ¾ cup of the marinade through a strainer into a 1-quart saucepan, bring to a boil over high heat, and cook for 1 minute. Baste the duck with it every 15 to 20 minutes. Reserve the remaining marinade.

5. Continue roasting the duck until an instant-read thermometer registers 155 degrees when inserted in the meaty part of the thigh or 160 degrees in the breast, about 20 to 30 minutes. Remove, allow the duck to rest until cool to the touch, and gently shred the meat.

6. Meanwhile, prepare the Plum *Pico de Gallo.*

7. In a large skillet pan, heat the oil over high heat until hot and shimmering. Add the duck pieces and quickly sauté until browned. Pour in ½ cup of the reserved marinade and sauté for 1 to 2 minutes more, or until the duck is glazed, stirring up any browned bits. Spoon the duck onto tortillas, and serve with cilantro sprigs and Plum *Pico de Gallo.*

Plum *Pico de Gallo*

In a bowl, stir together the plums, cilantro, onion, mint, *jalapeño,* and lime juice with sugar and salt to taste.

ROASTED QUAIL
Tacos

YIELD: 16 TACOS

Bobwhite quail are common in southern Mexico and especially the Yucatán. (If quail are unavailable, you could substitute squab.) This recipe uses a recado, *a colorful red-hued spice paste linked to the Mayan culture that originated here and whose members still populate the region.*

The Grilled Pineapple Black Olive Salsa is brimming with taste, texture, and color. The olives' saltiness and the smoky sweetness of the pineapple play beautifully against the quail. With fresh avocados in the mix, it's best to eat the salsa right away. To achieve the right charred-sweet flavor from the pineapple, don't cut the slices too thin or they will fall apart; too thick and the pineapple won't develop the desired consistency and flavor.

Grilled Pineapple Black Olive Salsa
(recipe follows)

8 cleaned quail, about 8 ounces each

2 *habañero* chiles

2 whole cloves

2 allspice berries

1 white onion, quartered

1 bay leaf

½ head garlic, roasted and peeled

Fine sea salt

Recado *(recipe follows)*

16 corn tortillas, warmed

1. Prepare the Grilled Pineapple Black Olive Salsa.

2. Preheat the oven to 350 degrees.

3. In a large pot, add the quail, *habañeros,* cloves, allspice, onion, bay leaf, garlic, and some salt. Bring to a boil, cover, reduce the heat, and simmer until the quail are just barely cooked through, 6 to 7 minutes. Using a slotted spoon, remove the quail and transfer to a heavy roasting pan. Strain and reserve the cooking liquid.

4. While the quail cooks, make the *recado.*

5. Brush the *recado* mixture over the quail and bake until golden brown, about 15 minutes. While the quail are baking, reduce the broth by half over high heat.

6. Remove the quail from the oven, cool slightly, and gently shred the meat. Toss with a little of the cooking liquid and fill the tortillas. Serve with Grilled Pineapple Black Olive Salsa.

3 (½-inch-thick) slices pineapple, cored

Blended oil, to brush the pineapple

10 oil-cured black olives, pitted and sliced

2 Roma tomatoes, cored, seeded,
    and cut into ¼-inch dice

1 firm ripe avocado, preferably Hass
    variety, peeled, seeded, and cut
    into ¼-inch dice

½ cup chopped red onion

¼ cup chopped fresh cilantro leaves

1½ teaspoons minced *jalapeño*,
    including seeds

¼ cup freshly squeezed lime juice

2 tablespoons extra-virgin olive oil

Fine sea salt

RECADO

5 whole peppercorns

2 whole cloves

1 teaspoon allspice berries

1 teaspoon coriander seeds

½ teaspoon dried oregano,
    preferably Mexican

1 (4-inch) stick cinnamon,
    preferably Mexican *canela*

10 cloves garlic, crushed

½ cup *achiote* paste

¼ cup rice vinegar, plus more
    as necessary

¼ cup freshly squeezed orange juice

¼ cup freshly squeezed lime juice

¼ cup olive oil

Grilled Pineapple Black Olive Salsa

1. Heat a grill until it's medium-hot. Lightly brush the pineapple with a little oil and grill until lightly browned with grill marks, about 3 minutes per side. Check often to see that the pineapple doesn't burn. Remove, let cool, and cut into ¼-inch dice.

2. In a bowl, toss together the pineapple, olives, tomatoes, avocado, onion, cilantro, and *jalapeño*. Pour on the lime juice and oil, toss again, and season to taste with salt.

Recado

In a clean coffee or spice grinder, grind the peppercorns, cloves, allspice, coriander, oregano, and cinnamon into a powder. Add them to a food processor along with the garlic, *achiote,* and vinegar; blend, adding more vinegar if needed to create a smooth paste. Add the orange juice, lime juice, and olive oil and blend.

TURKEY PICADILLO
Tacos

YIELD: 8 TACOS

While picadillo *filling is traditionally made with chopped or ground beef or pork, ground turkey and chicken (page 000) are easily substituted. The flavor is a contrast of sweet with salty. Serve the tacos with Apple-Cranberry Salsita (page 54) or your choice of salsas.*

Apple-Cranberry Salsita (page 54)

1 tablespoon blended oil

3 cloves garlic, minced

1 white onion, fairly finely chopped

1 *poblano* pepper, seeds and membranes
    removed, fairly finely chopped

1 cup tomato paste

¼ cup ground chile powder

1 pound ground turkey

¼ cup añejo tequila

2 cups canned tomato sauce

1 teaspoon salt

½ teaspoon Tabasco sauce

2 *serrano* chiles, minced

1 red potato (about 3 ounces),
    cut into ½-inch cubes and fried

½ cup dried cranberries

½ cup sliced green olives

½ cup toasted pecans

¼ cup dried cherries

Fine sea salt and freshly ground
    black pepper

8 corn tortillas, warmed

Crema, Greek yogurt,
    or crème fraîche, for garnish

1. Prepare the Apple-Cranberry Salsita.

2. In a large skillet, heat the oil, garlic, onion, and *poblano* pepper over medium-low heat. Cover and sweat until soft, 6 to 7 minutes, stirring occasionally. Stir in the tomato paste and chile powder.

3. Add the turkey and brown, breaking up the pieces with a wooden spatula. Pour in the tequila, bring to a boil over high heat, and stir up any browned cooking bits. Stir in the tomato sauce, salt, Tabasco sauce, *serrano* chiles, potato, cranberries, olives, pecans, and cherries. Return the mixture to a simmer and season to taste with salt and pepper.

4. Divide the filling among the tortillas. If desired, drizzle with *crema* and cilantro before serving.

BEEF, PORK, AND GAME

Tacos

BRISKET *Tacos with* GINGER PICKLED RED *Cabbage*

YIELD: 16 TACOS

The recipe for these intensely tasty tacos comes from my dear friend Alegría Sanchez. They are filled with brisket so tender it will remind you of the kind your abuelita, *or "grandma," used to make. The crunchy texture and sweet-tangy taste of Ginger Pickled Red Cabbage are a modern complement.*

Ginger Pickled Red Cabbage *(recipe follows)*

3 cloves garlic, crushed

¾ cup dry red wine

¼ cup chile powder

2 tablespoons rice vinegar

1 teaspoon cumin, preferably toasted whole and freshly ground

1 teaspoon dried oregano leaves, preferably Mexican

¼ teaspoon ground cinnamon, preferably Mexican *canela*

2 pounds center-cut beef brisket

Fine sea salt and freshly ground black pepper

2 medium white onions, thinly sliced

2 tablespoons blended oil, plus oil to fry the tortillas

5 Roma tomatoes, cored and diced

1 white onion, diced

1 *chipotle en adobo,* chopped

¼ cup chopped cilantro

16 corn tortillas, warmed

¾ cup crumbled *queso fresco*

1. Prepare the Ginger Pickled Red Cabbage.

2. For the Chile-Rubbed Brisket: In a large mixing bowl, whisk together the garlic, wine, chile powder, vinegar, cumin, oregano, and *canela*. Season the meat on both sides with salt and pepper.

3. Preheat the oven to 325 degrees.

4. Put the brisket in a roasting pan, cover with the chile mixture and onions, seal the pan tightly with heavy aluminum foil, and roast until the brisket is very tender when pierced with a fork, about 4 hours. Uncover and cook 1 hour longer to crisp the outside of the brisket. Remove from the oven, cool, tear into large shreds, and put into a large bowl.

5. In a large skillet, heat the 2 tablespoons of oil over medium-high heat. Add the tomatoes, onion, *chipotle,* and cilantro; cook until soft, stirring frequently. Season with salt and pepper to taste. Let cool and mix with the shredded beef.

6. Using a large skillet and working in batches, fry the tortillas in a little oil until just limp, not crisp, about 2 to 3 seconds. Fill with the beef and serve with a little of the Ginger Pickled Red Cabbage and drizzled with *queso fresco.* Serve extra cabbage on the side.

4 cups thinly sliced red cabbage

1 teaspoon fine sea salt

2 cups apple cider vinegar

1 tablespoon sugar

½ tablespoon grated fresh gingerroot

⅛ teaspoon ground allspice

⅛ teaspoon ground cinnamon

⅛ teaspoon freshly ground black pepper

Ginger Pickled Red Cabbage

1. In a large bowl, sprinkle the cabbage generously with salt. Let stand in a cool place for 30 minutes, drain, and transfer to a colander or vegetable steamer to drain for 30 minutes. Transfer to a plastic container.

2. In a small non-reactive saucepan, combine the vinegar, sugar, ginger, spices, and pepper; simmer for 10 minutes. Remove from the heat and pour over the cabbage. Cool, cover, and refrigerate.

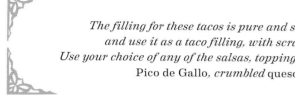

CHILE and BEER BRAISED BRISKET Tacos

YIELD: 16 TACOS

*The filling for these tacos is pure and simple comfort food. You can make it ahead
and use it as a taco filling, with scrambled eggs, or on a roll for sandwiches.
Use your choice of any of the salsas, toppings, and side dishes in this book. Shredded lettuce,
Pico de Gallo, crumbled queso fresco, and cilantro are classics.*

6 *ancho* chiles, stemmed and seeded

1 pound roasted and diced tomatoes

1 large white onion, coarsely chopped

4 cloves garlic, coarsely chopped

1 tablespoon *chile de árbol* powder

2 teaspoons ground cumin

Fine sea salt

1 cup Negra Modelo or
    other Mexican beer

2 pounds center-cut beef brisket

Freshly ground black pepper

1 tablespoon blended oil

16 corn tortillas, warmed

1. Tear the chiles into 1-inch pieces and put in a large bowl. Cover with hot water and soak until softened, at least 20 minutes. Drain.

2. Combine the tomatoes and their juices, the onion, garlic, chile powder, cumin, 1 teaspoon of salt, and the drained chiles into a food processor and process until smooth. Scrape the mixture into a large bowl and stir in the beer.

3. Preheat the oven to 300 degrees.

4. Season the brisket with salt and pepper. In a large roasting pan, heat the oil over medium heat. Add the brisket and brown on all sides, about 6 minutes total time. Pour the chile sauce over the meat and bring to a simmer. Cover tightly with aluminum foil, transfer to the oven, and braise for 3 hours. Remove the foil and continue braising until the meat is fall-apart tender, 45 minutes to 1 hour more.

5. Transfer the meat to a cutting board and pull it apart into long shreds using two forks. Stir the shredded meat back into the sauce. Spoon the mixture into the tortillas, garnish, and serve.

BEEF, PORK, *and* GAME *Tacos*

CORNED BEEF and CABBAGE Tacos

YIELD: 12 TACOS

*Why forgo your taco-lust on St. Paddy's Day? At Dos Caminos,
we love to celebrate all holidays, as with this Gaelic-inspired take on a taco filling.
We serve them with plenty of Guinness. If you happen to have leftover corned beef,
or want to buy it premade, it's all the easier to whip these unique tacos together.*

8 allspice berries

2 medium bay leaves, crumbled

2 fresh thyme sprigs

2 *ancho* chiles, stemmed and seeded

1 teaspoon black peppercorns

2 pounds center-cut beef brisket

3 cups beef broth

1 large white onion, cut in sixths

1 medium clove garlic, minced

12 corn tortillas, warmed

3 cups Spicy Cabbage Slaw *(recipe follows)*

Sliced pickled *jalapeños*

SPICY CABBAGE SLAW

1 head white cabbage, cored and
    thinly sliced

4 pickled *jalapeño* peppers, thinly sliced

2 carrots from pickled *jalapeños*,
    thinly sliced

1 red onion, thinly sliced

½ bunch cilantro, julienned

½ cup juice from pickled *jalapeños*

½ cup freshly squeezed grapefruit juice

¼ cup freshly squeezed lime juice

Fine sea salt

1. Combine the allspice, bay leaves, thyme, *ancho* chiles, and peppercorns in a doubled 8-inch square of cheesecloth and tie it tightly to keep the herbs and spices inside. Add it to a 12-quart pot along with the brisket and broth. Pour in enough water to cover the brisket, add the onion and garlic, and bring to a boil. Reduce the heat to low, cover, and simmer for 2 hours until tender.

2. Remove the corned beef to a platter, cover with foil, and keep warm in a very low oven or warming drawer.

3. When you're ready to serve, cut the corned beef across the grain into very thin slices and distribute the meat evenly among the tortillas. Top with Spicy Cabbage Slaw and sprinkle with *jalapeños*.

Spicy Cabbage Slaw

In a large bowl, combine the cabbage, *jalapeño* peppers, carrot, onion, cilantro, *jalapeño* juice, grapefruit juice, and lime juice. Season to taste with salt. Let stand 30 minutes. Juice should taste salty and sweet, like pickling liquid.

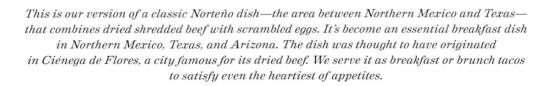

NUEVO *León* STYLE DRIED BEEF and SCRAMBLED EGG *Tacos*

YIELD: 12 TACOS

This is our version of a classic Norteño dish—the area between Northern Mexico and Texas— that combines dried shredded beef with scrambled eggs. It's become an essential breakfast dish in Northern Mexico, Texas, and Arizona. The dish was thought to have originated in Ciénega de Flores, a city famous for its dried beef. We serve it as breakfast or brunch tacos to satisfy even the heartiest of appetites.

½ cup *Pico de Gallo* (page 39)

Guacamole, for garnish (page 44)

1 teaspoon blended oil

1 pound leftover Chile and Beer Braised Brisket (page 177) or purchased cooked brisket, shredded as finely as possible

1 dozen large eggs, beaten

Fine sea salt and freshly ground black pepper

12 (6-inch) flour tortillas

12 slices aged cheddar cheese

4 limes, cut into quarters

1. Prepare the *Pico de Gallo* and Guacamole.

2. In a very large skillet, heat the oil over medium-high heat. Add the brisket and brown well, stirring often. Stir in the *Pico de Gallo* and cook for 1 minute to reduce the liquid slightly. Add the eggs, season with salt and pepper, and stir until the eggs are just set.

3. Meanwhile, heat a griddle or large skillet over high heat. Lay the tortillas on the griddle, heat one side, turn, put a slice of cheese on each, and let it melt slightly.

4. Fill the tortillas with brisket and fold in half.

5. To serve, line up two or three tacos on each plate with lime "bookends" and serve with additional *Pico de Gallo* and Guacamole.

TAMARIND *Braised* SHORT RIB *Tacos*

YIELD: 16 TACOS

Short ribs need long, slow braising to soften the meat and develop rich flavors, so this sweet and tangy version made with tamarind is best prepared ahead of time. You should have enough leftovers for the Gorditas de Res *on page 184.* Elote de Calle, Mexico City–Style Street Corn (page 224), *would be a great addition to this meal.*

8 meaty beef short ribs, about 6 pounds

¼ cup kosher salt

6 canned *chipotles en adobo*,
   plus 1 additional *chipotle*, chopped

1 large white onion, diced,
   and 1 small white onion, diced

1 large carrot, diced

1 bay leaf

1 cup balsamic vinegar

1 cup dry white wine

½ cup firmly packed dark brown sugar

1 tablespoon chopped garlic

1 cup tamarind paste

2 tablespoons blended oil

5 Roma tomatoes, cored and diced

Fine sea salt and freshly ground
   black pepper

16 corn tortillas, warmed

Crema, Greek yogurt,
   or crème fraîche, for garnish

½ cup chopped cilantro,
   plus 2 tablespoons for garnish

¼ cup toasted sesame seeds, for garnish

1. Heat the oven to 350 degrees.

2. Season the short ribs generously with salt, lay them side by side in a large heavy roasting pan, and scatter the six *chipotles en adobo,* the large onion, carrot, and bay leaf on top of the meat.

3. In a small bowl, stir together the vinegar, wine, brown sugar, and garlic; pour over the short ribs. In a separate bowl, whisk the tamarind paste into 1 cup of hot water to dissolve it a little, then combine it with the vinegar-wine liquid and pour into the pan. The liquid should come about three-quarters of the way up the sides of the short ribs. Add more water, if necessary.

4. Cover the pan tightly with foil and again with a second layer of foil. Transfer to the oven and braise until the meat falls apart when poked with a fork, 3 to 3½ hours, removing the foil to check that the ribs are tender. Using tongs, carefully remove the ribs to a platter, cover, and set aside to cool at room temperature.

5. Strain the liquid through a fine strainer into a large container. Chill for at least 1 hour so the fat rises to the surface and forms a solid chunk. Remove and discard.

6. In a large, deep skillet over high heat, bring the braising liquid to a boil and reduce to about 3½ cups. Return the short ribs to the pan, turn the heat down to medium-low, and simmer until the ribs start to become glazed and sticky with the sauce, 50 to 55 minutes, turning with the tongs. Remove from the heat, pull the meat off the bones, and shred it with two forks. (The recipe may be made several days ahead to this point.) Keep warm if you're serving right away.

7. In a large skillet, heat the oil over medium-high heat. Add the tomatoes, remaining onion, remaining *chipotle,* and cilantro; cook, stirring, until soft, about 6 minutes. Season with salt and pepper to taste, and mix with the shredded beef. Spoon the filling into the tortillas, drizzle with *crema,* cilantro, and sesame seeds, and serve.

BEEF-STUFFED *Gorditas* with *Habañero Salsa*

YIELD: 6 (4-INCH) GORDITAS

Gorditas, or "little fat ones," are thick, griddled tacos typically filled with stewed meats like beef, pork, or chicken. They may also be made with black beans and/or cheese. Here I pair them with really hot Habañero *Salsa, but use a salsa of your own choice, if you prefer. In the areas around Lake Pátzcuaro, the dough for* gorditas *is made with blue cornmeal, as it is here.*

1 cup Tamarind Braised Short Ribs (reserved from recipe on page 183)

Habañero Salsa *(recipe follows)*

2 cups blue cornmeal

¼ cup all-purpose flour

1 teaspoon baking powder

1 teaspoon fine sea salt

Blended oil (about 3 cups) for frying

¼ cup crumbled *Cotija* cheese

½ cup thinly sliced red cabbage

1. Prepare the Tamarind Braised Short Ribs and *Habañero* Salsa.

2. In a large bowl, mix the cornmeal, flour, baking powder, and salt together. Add 1½ cups of water and stir until the dough is smooth. Form the dough into walnut-sized balls, cover, and set aside.

3. Moisten a cloth napkin and spread it out on a flat surface. Roll each ball of dough in the moistened palms of your hands until smooth, press your thumb into the center of each ball to make a dimple, and fill it with a tablespoon of braised short ribs. Roll again to cover the short ribs and put the balls on the napkin. Cover each ball with a plastic bag and press down to flatten it into a ½-inch disk.

4. Fill a large cast-iron skillet about halfway up with oil and heat over medium-high heat to 375 degrees when measured on an instant-read thermometer. Slide a few patties into the hot oil and fry until golden brown and crispy, about 1½ minutes per side. Don't crowd. Remove with a slotted spoon or tongs to drain on paper towels. As soon as they are cool enough to handle, make a slit on the side of each disk and stuff with 1 teaspoon of crumbled cheese and a little cabbage, drizzle with 1 teaspoon of *Habañero* Salsa, and serve.

2 orange *habañero* chiles, cut in half

½ Roma tomato

1 shallot, cut in half

1 clove garlic

1½ bay leaves

1 small carrot, cut in half lengthwise

½ yellow bell pepper

1½ cups white vinegar

Fine sea salt

Habañero Salsa

In a medium-sized non-reactive pan, combine the chiles, tomato, shallot, garlic, bay leaves, carrot, bell pepper, vinegar, and 1½ cups water; bring to a boil. Cook until the peppers are just tender, about 10 minutes. Strain and transfer the solids to the jar of an electric blender, reserving the liquid. Puree until the salsa is smooth, adding just enough liquid to blend, about 2 tablespoons. Season to taste with salt and cool.

CHEF'S TIPS:

Habañeros are one of the hottest chiles and not for timid taste buds. Removing the seeds and membranes will tame the fire a little. Beyond the heat is a distinct fruitiness that adds a wonderful spark to almost anything.
Besides Gorditas de Res, this salsa is an excellent dip for tortilla chips or spooned on a simple piece of grilled fish.
It's also a nice sauce to combine with dishes that include fruits, like mango, orange, or pineapple.

Cascabel CHILE MARINATED Carne Asada TACOS WITH CARAMELIZED ONIONS, Pico de Gallo, AND Cotija CHEESE

YIELD: 12 TACOS

In Mexico, carne asada *usually refers to steak that's pounded flat, marinated, and cooked* a la plancha—*on a flat griddle or* comal—*to sear the outside of the meat. It's then sliced and used in tacos, enchiladas, burritos, and so forth. Basically it's like barbecuing and just as popular. Since most people don't have a* comal *at home, I suggest cooking the meat on a grill or in a cast-iron skillet on the stovetop.*

Cascabel chiles have a toasty, nutty red chile flavor but mild to medium heat. This most traditional of tacos is more exciting because the meat is first marinated, creating a very flavorful filling.

6 *cascabel* chiles, stemmed and seeded

1 *chile de árbol*, stemmed and seeded

½ cup reserved cooking liquid from soaking the chiles

1 small white onion, quartered

3 cloves garlic

½ cup apple cider vinegar

¼ cup Maggi sauce or Worcestershire sauce

2 tablespoons freshly squeezed lime juice

½ tablespoon dried oregano, preferably Mexican

1 tablespoon kosher salt, divided

1½ pounds (1-inch-thick) sirloin steak, butterflied (or ask the butcher to do this)

Pico de Gallo (page 39)

½ recipe Guacamole (page 44)

Kosher salt and freshly ground black pepper

12 corn tortillas, warmed

½ cup grated *Cotija* cheese, for garnish

Salsa of choice

1. Preheat the oven to 350 degrees.

2. Make the marinade: Cook the chiles in a dry skillet over medium heat until you can smell the toasty aroma, 2 to 3 minutes, shaking frequently. Transfer them to a medium saucepan, cover with water, and bring to a simmer. Remove the pan from the heat, cool, and drain. Reserve the soaking liquid.

3. Meanwhile, roast the onion on an ungreased baking sheet until brown, 10 to 12 minutes.

4. Combine the chiles with the garlic, vinegar, Maggi, lime juice, oregano, and 1 teaspoon of the salt in the jar of an electric blender. Puree until smooth, adding some of the soaking liquid if needed to help the blades turn easily. In a large bowl, toss the steak with the marinade, making sure it is well coated. Cover and refrigerate for 8 hours or overnight.

5. About 1 hour before cooking the meat, prepare the *Pico de Gallo* and Guacamole.

6. Heat the barbecue until hot. Remove the steak from the marinade and discard the marinade. Season the meat on both sides with salt and pepper and grill to the desired degree of doneness, 2 to 3 minutes per side for medium-rare, turning once. Remove to a cutting board, let rest for 1 to 2 minutes, and then slice crosswise into ½-inch-wide strips.

7. While the steak is cooking, wrap the tortillas in aluminum foil and heat on the grill for about 5 minutes.

8. To serve, spoon 1 tablespoon of Guacamole onto each warm tortilla. Add the *carne asada,* then garnish with 1 to 2 tablespoons of *Pico de Gallo* and about 1 teaspoon *Cotija* cheese. Serve 2 tacos per person with salsa on the side.

Michoacán-Style BEEF TENDERLOIN TIP Tacos

YIELD: 16 TACOS

Michoacán is a state in southwestern Mexico that borders the Pacific Ocean.
Locals are known for slowly simmering meats (often in lard) in large copper cauldrons until the pieces
are crispy on the outside and tender inside. Most famously, there are carnitas (see page 146).
I adapted the idea to beef tenderloin tips with bacon.
The pieces are juicy, tender, and more practical than using filet mignon.

2 tablespoons unsalted butter

2 tablespoons olive oil

2 medium white onions, halved and sliced
   on the diagonal, plus 1 small onion,
   finely chopped

7 *serrano* chiles, seeded and cut
   into thin strips

3 medium tomatoes, cored and
   finely chopped

Fine sea salt and freshly ground
   black pepper

½ pound sliced bacon, finely chopped

1½ cups mixed wild mushrooms,
   cleaned and sliced

1 *chile de árbol*, sliced into thin rings

2 pounds fillet of beef tips,
   cut into 2 x ½-inch strips

16 corn tortillas, warmed

2 *jalapeños*, seeded and cut
   into thin strips

½ cup chopped fresh cilantro

1. Heat a large, heavy skillet over medium-high heat. Add the butter and oil, stir in the sliced onion and chiles, and cook until the onion is golden, about 15 minutes, stirring frequently.

2. Add the tomatoes, season lightly with salt and pepper, and simmer uncovered until the tomatoes break down, the sauce thickens, and the fat rises to surface, about 30 minutes, stirring occasionally. Skim off the fat for cooking; reserve both the fat and the sauce in separate bowls.

3. Wipe out the pan and heat over medium-high heat until hot. Add the bacon and fry until crisp, turning often. Remove the pieces to paper towels to drain.

4. Add enough of the reserved fat to have 2 tablespoons of fat in the skillet, stir in the remaining onion along with the mushrooms and *chiles de árbol,* and sauté until golden brown, about 5 minutes. Scrape into a bowl.

5. Add the beef to the skillet and brown on all sides, 4 to 5 minutes. Season lightly with salt and pepper, remove to a plate, tent with foil, and keep warm.

6. Return the onion-mushroom mixture to the skillet along with the beef. Add the sauce and bacon, cooking over medium heat for about 5 minutes. Divide the beef among the tortillas, sprinkle with *jalapeños* and cilantro, and serve.

Carne Parrillada TACOS WITH Chiles Rajas

YIELD: 16 TACOS

*Throughout Mexico, there's a long tradition of serving mixed grills
that include different kinds of meats as well as poultry and even vegetables.
In town squares everywhere, the air is perfumed with the wonderful aroma of charred foods
on weekends. These tacos combine the flavors and textures of grilled hanger steak, bacon,
crumbled cheese like* Menonita *(see the sidebar), and tri-colored* Chiles Rajas.
At Dos Caminos, each plate includes My Refried Beans (page 228) and Elote de Calle,
*Mexico's tempting street-style corn on the cob (page 224).
The ears can be grilled along with the steak.*

Chiles Rajas (recipe follows)

2½ pounds hanger steak, trimmed

2 tablespoons Maldon or
    other coarse sea salt

1 tablespoon crushed red chile flakes

1 tablespoon dried oregano,
    preferably Mexican

2 teaspoons blended oil

1 medium white onion, sliced

Fine sea salt and freshly ground
    black pepper

½ pound sliced bacon, chopped

1 pound crumbled or shredded *Menonita,
    queso blanco,* or Monterey Jack cheese

16 corn tortillas, warmed

Guacamole (page 44)

Pico de Gallo (page 39)

1. Prepare the *Chiles Rajas*.

2. Slice the steak across the grain into ½-inch-thick slices and flatten slightly with a meat pounder. Combine the salt, chile flakes, and oregano; sprinkle on the slices. Transfer the meat to a covered container and refrigerate for 6 hours or overnight.

3. Heat the oil in a heavy skillet over medium-high heat. Add the onion and sauté until golden brown and caramelized. Scrape into a bowl and set aside.

4. Heat a grill or large heavy skillet to medium-high. Cook the beef slices until medium-rare, 2 to 3 minutes, turning once. Remove and season with salt and pepper to taste.

5. Meanwhile, in the same skillet used for the onion, fry the bacon over medium heat until cooked through. Add the cooked onion, steak, *Chiles Rajas,* and cheese; toss until the cheese is melted.

6. Spoon the mixture into the tortillas, top with Guacamole and *Pico de Gallo*, and serve.

1 tablespoon olive oil

½ medium red onion, thinly sliced

2 cloves garlic, thinly sliced

1 red bell pepper, roasted, peeled,
   seeded, and cut into thin strips

1 yellow bell pepper, roasted, peeled,
   seeded, and cut into thin strips

1 *poblano* chile, roasted, peeled, seeded,
   and cut into thin strips

2 tablespoons sherry vinegar

1 tablespoon freshly squeezed lime juice

½ tablespoon Maggi sauce
   or Worcestershire sauce

½ teaspoon kosher salt

Chiles Rajas (Three-Colored Pickled Peppers)

In a large skillet, heat the olive oil over medium-high heat. Add the onion and sauté until lightly browned, about 5 minutes. Add the garlic and sauté for 1 minute more, stirring frequently. Stir in the peppers and chile strips and mix thoroughly. Pour in the vinegar, lime juice, and Maggi sauce, lower the heat, and simmer for 5 minutes, stirring occasionally. Season to taste with salt and refrigerate.

BEEF *Picadillo* TACOS

YIELD: 16 TACOS

When you want familiar-tasting tacos, yet a version that will satisfy even sophisticated palates, try my picadillo *filling. It's a simple yet flavorful mixture of ground beef and spices.* Picadillo *means "chopped" or "ground" in Spanish. Dress these up with thinly sliced lettuce, shredded cheese, chopped onions, and salsa.*

1 tablespoon blended oil

2½ pounds lean ground beef

1 white onion, cut into small dice

¼ cup minced garlic

¼ cup chopped shallots

1 tablespoon *pasilla de Oaxaca* chile powder

1 tablespoon Hungarian sweet paprika

½ tablespoon ground cayenne pepper

¼ cup tomato paste

Fine sea salt

16 corn tortillas, warmed

JALAPEÑO MINT SALSITA

¼ cup apple cider vinegar

¼ cup *piloncillo* or turbinado sugar

1 tablespoon blended oil

¼ cup minced white onion

4 *jalapeños*, roasted, peeled, seeded, and diced

Fine sea salt

1 tablespoon freshly squeezed lime juice

¼ cup fresh mint leaves, cut in chiffonade

In a large pot, heat the oil over medium-high heat. Add the beef, onion, garlic, and shallots; cook until the onion is golden brown, 5 to 7 minutes. Stir in the chile powder, paprika, cayenne pepper, and tomato paste, cooking for about 5 more minutes. Season to taste with salt and divide among the tortillas. Serve with your choice of toppings and salsas.

VARIATIONS: Try ground lamb drizzled with scallions and Spicy Mint *Crema* made with Greek yogurt (page 88). Or you can make venison *picadillo* with finely chopped or ground venison—or, if you are in the Sonoran Desert, giant mule deer—served with *Jalapeño* Mint Salsita (below).

Jalapeño Mint Salsita

In a small saucepan, combine the vinegar and *piloncillo* and simmer until the sugar is dissolved. In a medium-sized skillet over medium heat, add the oil and onion, partially cover, and sweat until translucent. Add the *jalapeños* and *piloncillo*-vinegar syrup and simmer until the mixture binds together. Season to taste with salt and cool. Finish by folding in the lime juice and fresh mint.

BEEF TONGUE *Tacos* in FRESH TOMATO SERRANO CHILE *Salsa*

YIELD: 16 TACOS

Mexicans eat every part of an animal, and waste of any kind is considered a sin. Slowly simmered tongue that's sliced and cubed is a very popular taco filling. The sweet meat is nicely accented with tangy-bold Fresh Tomato Serrano Chile Salsa. It's a favorite of my longtime friend and fellow chef Scott Linquist.

3–4 pounds beef tongue, excess fat trimmed

12 peppercorns

6 cloves garlic

1 white onion, coarsely chopped

6 sprigs thyme

6 sprigs fresh marjoram

2 bay leaves

¼ cup kosher salt

Fresh Tomato *Serrano* Chile Salsa
(recipe follows)

16 corn tortillas, warmed

FRESH TOMATO *SERRANO* CHILE SALSA

½ pound Roma tomatoes, cored, seeded, and finely chopped

⅝ cup finely chopped white onion

⅜ cup chopped cilantro

2–3 *serrano* chiles, seeded and finely chopped

Fine sea salt

1. In a large saucepan, cover the tongue with cold water. Add the peppercorns, garlic, onion, thyme, marjoram, bay leaves, and salt; bring to a boil over high heat. Reduce the heat and simmer until the meat is tender, about 3 hours.

2. Meanwhile, prepare the Fresh Tomato *Serrano* Chile Salsa.

3. Cool the tongue in the broth. Peel and return it to the broth to cool completely. When it's cold, cut it into bite-sized cubes, fill the tortillas, and serve with *Salsa Roja Cruda*.

Fresh Tomato *Serrano* Chile Salsa

YIELD: 2 CUPS

In a non-reactive bowl, combine the tomatoes, onion, cilantro, and chiles. Season to taste with salt.

TRIPE *Tacos*

YIELD: 16 TACOS

Tripe tacos are among the most beloved street foods in Mexico. Until you taste cooked tripe—the pieces are deliciously crunchy on the outside and soft inside—the idea may be kind of off-putting. Once you try them, however, I believe you'll be a convert, as I was. They are especially appealing when served in tortillas made into cones with Herbed Salsa Verde*, a squeeze of lime, cilantro, and Guacamole. Although this looks like a lot of tripe, when tripe cooks, it shrinks dramatically.*

Herbed *Salsa Verde* (recipe follows)

4 pounds tripe, cleaned, rinsed, and drained

2 tablespoons blended oil

Fine sea salt

16 corn tortillas

1 large white onion, finely chopped

12 corn tortillas, warmed

½ recipe Guacamole (page 44)

½ cup chopped cilantro

2 limes, cut in quarters

HERBED *SALSA VERDE*

1 cup baby arugula leaves

¼ bunch flat-leaf parsley, coarsely chopped

Leaves from 2 sprigs marjoram, coarsely chopped

Leaves from 2 sprigs basil, coarsely chopped

Zest of 1 orange

1 anchovy fillet, rinsed well and patted dry

1 clove garlic

½ teaspoon freshly ground pepper

¼ teaspoon fine sea salt

¼ cup extra-virgin olive oil

1. Prepare the Herbed *Salsa Verde.*

2. Fill a large pot with water and heat over medium-high heat. Add the tripe, cover, and simmer until soft, 50 minutes to an hour. Using a slotted spoon, remove the tripe to paper towels to drain. Cut into 1-inch cubes.

3. In a large, heavy skillet, heat the oil over medium-high heat. Add the tripe and fry until golden brown but with the insides still soft, about 8 minutes, turning the pieces often. Remove to paper towels and season with salt.

4. Roll each tortilla into a triangular cone and fasten the side with a toothpick. Fold about an inch at the bottom over. Spoon a generous tablespoon of Guacamole in the bottom of each cone. Divide the tripe among the cones, ladle on some Herbed *Salsa Verde,* drizzle with cilantro, and squeeze on some lime juice.

Herbed *Salsa Verde*

In a food processor, pulse the arugula, parsley, marjoram, basil, orange zest, anchovy, garlic, pepper, salt, and olive oil until blended and chunky-smooth.

MEXICAN HOT DOG
Tacos

YIELD: 10 TACOS

In 1943, two enterprising Americans set up a hot dog cart at the central bullring in Mexico City, and the country's passion for perros calientes *was born. By the '50s, there was a cart selling bacon-wrapped hot dogs with all the trimmings in Mexico City's Parque de la Alameda. Today you will find hot dogs served that way all over the country.*

As a teenager in the '80s, my family and I visited Tijuana where I had my first TJ Dog: crisp, thin-sliced bacon wrapped around a sizzling dog, tucked inside a warm tortilla, topped with melted cheese and pickled jalapeños. *I still love them.*

Buy good-quality hot dogs (we use Kobe beef in the restaurants), but really any kind works.

1 cup Roasted Tomato *Chile de Árbol* Salsa (page 34)

10 hot dogs

3 ounces sharp cheddar cheese

½ cup canned or jarred pickled *jalapeños*

20 thin slices smoked bacon

10 (8-inch) flour tortillas

1. Prepare the Roasted Tomato *Chile de Árbol* Salsa.

2. With a sharp knife, cut the hot dogs open lengthwise, making a 2½-inch-long slit, leaving the ends intact.

3. Using a vegetable peeler, peel the cheese into strips. Divide the cheese among the hot dogs. Add two or three *jalapeño* slices to each, wrap in two slices of bacon, and secure with toothpicks.

4. If you'll be grilling, heat your barbecue to medium-hot and warm the tortillas. Otherwise, warm the tortillas in a preheated 350-degree oven or toaster oven for 10 minutes.

5. Lay the hot dogs on the grill cut-side up. When the cheese melts, rotate the hot dogs 15 to 25 degrees, to cook each side, about 8 minutes total. If you're cooking in the preheated 350-degree oven, bake the hot dogs for 15 to 18 minutes. Remove the hot dogs with tongs, place each in a warm tortilla, remove the toothpicks, top with Roasted Tomato *Chile de Árbol* Salsa, and roll up.

Cochinita Pibil
TACOS

YIELD: 14 TACOS

Early Mayans on the Yucatán Peninsula slowly roasted young suckling pigs, or cochinitas, *wrapped in banana leaves, in deep pits until they became succulent and fork-tender. Before the meat was buried (*pibil *means "buried" in the local dialect), it was marinated in an acidic liquid that traditionally included bitter oranges and annatto-based* achiote *paste to add flavor and impart the characteristic orangey-red color.*

Lacking Seville oranges, a deep pit, and a whole young pig for this classic dish, my slow-roasted version, made with pork butt cut from the shoulder, produces an aromatic and deliciously tender taco filling. Spicy-tangy Habañero *Pickled Red Onions make a tasty and tangy foil for the meat. If you have a backyard, use a "Caja China" roasting box to make a great pibil.*

Banana leaves, as needed

2 cups freshly squeezed orange juice

1 cup freshly squeezed lime juice

1 cup *achiote* paste

3 tablespoons honey

1 tablespoon kosher salt

2½ pounds boneless pork butt,
   cut into cubes

2 oranges, quartered

2 carrots, cut in large dice

1½ white onions, diced

1 small stalk celery, cut in large dice

1 tablespoon whole black peppercorns

3 bay leaves

4 cups chicken stock

Fine sea salt

Habañero Pickled Red Onions (page 78)

14 corn tortillas, warmed

¾ cup thinly sliced scallions, mostly white
   parts or cilantro, for garnish

1. Preheat the oven to 250 degrees. Line a deep roasting pan with foil. Add enough banana leaves to ensure they extend over the edges of the pan and can be turned back over the meat to cover it.

2. In a small bowl, blend the orange and lime juices, *achiote* paste, honey, and salt. Add the pork and turn to coat evenly with the marinade. Add the oranges, carrots, onions, celery, peppercorns, and bay leaves. Pour in the stock and season with salt.

3. Fold the leaves over so the pork is fully covered. Transfer to the oven and roast until the meat is very tender, 12 to 14 hours.

4. Meanwhile, prepare the *Habañero* Pickled Red Onions.

5. Remove the meat from the oven, cool, and shred with two forks. Add enough of the pan juices to keep the meat moist. Divide the meat among the tortillas, add some *Habañero* Pickled Red Onions, drizzle with scallions, and serve.

PORK SHANK *Tacos with* PICKLED *Red* CABBAGE

YIELD: 16 TACOS

Meltingly tender, perfectly spiced pork shanks make tacos that will cause you and your guests to swoon with pleasure. Although the ingredient list is long, this is really a simple recipe that yields juicy morsels of pork. You can also try this with lamb shanks.

I first had these tacos at El Bosque, in Mexico City. It's a true old school cantina because women aren't allowed in the bar; they can only enter the dining room if accompanied by a man.

12 cloves garlic

4 tomatillos, husked, rinsed, and quartered

2 medium white onions, coarsely chopped

4 tablespoons olive or blended oil, divided

Fine sea salt and freshly ground
    black pepper

12 black peppercorns

6 bay leaves

2 cloves

2 pieces star anise

2 teaspoons dried oregano,
    preferably Mexican

2 teaspoons cumin seeds, toasted

6 dried *ancho* chiles, stems and seeds
    removed, toasted

6 dried *guajillo* chiles, stems and seeds
    removed, toasted

1 cup apple cider vinegar

1 cup freshly squeezed orange juice

3 or 4 large fresh banana leaves

5 medium-sized, bone-in pork shanks

2 cups chicken stock

16 corn tortillas, warmed

Salsa Roja Cruda (Fresh Tomato *Serrano*
    Chile Salsa) (page 194)

1 cup Pickled Red Cabbage *(recipe follows)*

1 cup crumbled *queso fresco*, for garnish

1. Preheat the oven to 400 degrees.

2. Toss the garlic, tomatillos, and onions with 1 tablespoon of the oil, season with salt and pepper, spread on a baking sheet, and roast until lightly browned, about 15 minutes, turning occasionally. Set aside.

3. Grind the peppercorns, bay leaves, cloves, anise, oregano, and cumin in a clean coffee mill or spice grinder.

4. In a medium-sized saucepan, cover the toasted chiles with water and bring to a simmer. Remove the pan from the heat and set aside for a few minutes to cool. In the jar of an electric blender, combine the tomatillo mixture along with the chiles, vinegar, and orange juice; puree until smooth. Transfer to a bowl, stir in the peppercorn bay leaf mixture, and set aside.

5. Line a roasting pan with banana leaves or parchment paper. Season the shanks with salt and pepper, rub with half of the marinade, lay them in the pan, and marinate for 1 hour to overnight. Pour the remaining marinade over the top.

6. Before cooking, return the meat to room temperature, about 45 minutes. Meanwhile, preheat the oven to 350 degrees. Pour in the chicken stock. Fold the banana leaves over the meat, cover with aluminum foil, and seal on all sides. Bake until the meat is fork-tender and easily pulled away from the bone, 2 to 3 hours.

7. While the pork cooks, prepare the *Salsa Roja Cruda* and Pickled Red Cabbage.

8. Remove the meat from the oven, transfer it to a bowl, and let it cool. Pull the meat from the bones in medium-sized pieces. Strain the cooking liquid into a bowl.

9. To serve, heat a tablespoon of the remaining oil in a large skillet over medium-high heat. Add the pork pieces and brown on all sides, turning often, and adding more oil as necessary. Ladle about 1 cup of the cooking liquid onto the meat to moisten. Spoon the pieces into the tortillas and serve with *queso fresco, Salsa Roja Cruda,* and Pickled Red Cabbage.

PICKLED RED CABBAGE

2 cloves garlic, thinly sliced

1 head red cabbage, cored and shaved

1 small red onion, thinly sliced lengthwise

1 *jalapeño*, seeds and membranes removed, thinly sliced lengthwise

Leaves from 2 sprigs oregano

2 cups apple cider vinegar

1 teaspoon sugar

Fine sea salt

Pickled Red Cabbage

Combine the garlic, cabbage, onion, *jalapeño*, and oregano in a large non-reactive bowl. Stir in the vinegar and sugar; season to taste with salt and let stand for at least 2 hours to overnight before serving.

Grilled ARAB-STYLE Tacos with Jalapeño YOGURT

YIELD: 8 TACOS

Arab-style tacos are said to be an adaptation of the spit-roasted meats prepared by Arabic-speaking immigrants who came to Mexico during the 19th and early 20th centuries. Many settled in Puebla and Mexico City, and both regions claim them as their own. Traditionally, these tacos are made with layered pork marinated in a secret recipe that varies from vendor to vendor, then skewered on an upright spit, and served on thick flour tortillas or pita breads. Our tacos are grilled and served with tangy, spicy Jalapeño *Yogurt.* Jocoque, *or strained Greek-style yogurt, also came to Mexico with Arab immigrants.*

16 ounces Greek yogurt

Juice of 5 limes

6 cloves garlic

1 bunch flat-leaf parsley

Leaves from 1 sprig mint

Leaves from 1 sprig thyme

1 tablespoon dried oregano, preferably Mexican

1 teaspoon ground cumin

¼ cup olive oil

2 pounds pork loin, cut into slices

8 thick flour tortillas or 6-inch pita breads

Jocoque (Jalapeño Yogurt; *recipe follows)*

JALAPEÑO YOGURT

1 cup Greek yogurt

2–3 seeded *jalapeños,* minced

2 cloves garlic, minced

2 tablespoons finely chopped fresh cilantro

1 teaspoon freshly grated ginger

1 teaspoon ground coriander

1 teaspoon ground cumin

Fine sea salt and freshly ground black pepper

1. In the jar of an electric blender, combine the yogurt, lime juice, garlic, parsley, mint, thyme, oregano, cumin, and olive oil. Puree until smooth. Put the pork in a flat, non-reactive container, pour on the marinade, and refrigerate overnight or for at least 8 hours.

2. Prepare the *Jalapeño* Yogurt.

3. Heat a barbecue to medium or heat a large cast-iron skillet over medium-high heat.

4. Remove the pork from the marinade, place directly on the grill without blotting, and cook to medium, about 4 or 5 minutes each side, turning once. Serve wrapped in thick tortillas drizzled with *Jalapeño* Yogurt.

Jalapeño Yogurt

In a small bowl, whisk together the yogurt, *jalapeños,* garlic, cilantro, ginger, coriander, and cumin. Season with salt and black pepper to taste.

CARNITAS *Tacos with* SERRANO CHILE *Salsa*

YIELD: 16 TACOS

Pork simmered in Coca-Cola, orange juice, and condensed milk sounds unusual, but it's common in Mexico and practically a religion in Michoacán. I think you'll discover it's quite delicious. Along with the orangey-citrus flavor, the finished meat retains a hint of caramel from the cola and creaminess from the milk.

8 pounds lard

4 pounds bone-in pork butt, cut into large cubes

1 cup freshly squeezed orange juice

1 cup Coca-Cola

1 (14-ounce) can sweetened condensed milk

10 bay leaves

2 sprigs fresh thyme

2 tablespoons whole peppercorns

1 large stick cinnamon, preferably Mexican *canela*

Fine sea salt

Serrano Chile Salsa *(recipe follows)*

16 corn tortillas, warmed

1½ cups shredded white or red cabbage, for garnish

½ cilantro leaves, for garnish

SERRANO CHILE SALSA

½ cup apple cider vinegar

½ tablespoon sugar

2 whole allspice berries

2 tablespoons blended oil

½ cup minced white onions

8–10 *serrano* chiles, roasted, peeled, seeded, and diced

½ tablespoon fine sea salt

2 tablespoons freshly squeezed lime juice

1 cup chopped cilantro

1. Preheat the oven to 300 degrees.

2. In a large, deep pot, melt the lard. Add the pork, orange juice, Coca-Cola, condensed milk, bay leaves, thyme, peppercorns, *canela,* and 2 teaspoons salt; bring to a simmer. Transfer the pot to the oven and cook until tender, 1 to 2 hours.

3. Meanwhile, prepare the *Serrano* Chile Salsa.

4. Remove the pork from the oven. Heat on top of the stove over high heat to brown the outside; taste to adjust the salt level. Cool slightly and, using two forks, shred the meat into large chunks.

5. To serve, spoon the meat into the tortillas, top with a little cabbage and cilantro, and drizzle with *Serrano* Chile Salsa.

Serrano Chile Salsa

1. In small saucepan, combine the vinegar, sugar, and allspice; simmer until the sugar dissolves. Set aside.

2. Heat the oil in a medium-sized skillet over medium heat. Stir in the onions and cook until translucent, about 4 minutes. Add the *serranos,* allspice-vinegar syrup, and salt; gently simmer until the mixture binds together, 8 to 10 minutes. Cool, fold in the lime juice and cilantro, scrape into a food processor, and process until blended but still slightly chunky. Taste to adjust the salt, if needed.

MEATBALL *Tacos in* *Chipotle* SAUCE

YIELD: 16 TACOS

Meatballs, popular around the world, are known in Mexico as albondigas *and are often served in soup. Here I use a very flavorful combination of beef, pork, and veal to give the meat a rich flavor. A friend of my mom's from Milan, Italy, who was a wonderful cook, taught me how to make meatballs; I use her secret recipe along with a few secrets of my own. Use extra* Chipotle *Salsa for sandwiches and other tacos.*

Chipotle Salsa (page 35)

1 cup chicken stock

6 cloves garlic, coarsely chopped

1 large white onion, coarsely chopped

1 bunch flat-leaf parsley, chopped,
  plus a few reserved chopped leaves
  for garnish

1 pound ground beef

1 pound ground pork

1 pound ground veal

3 large eggs, lightly beaten

1 cup grated *Cotija* cheese, or substitute
  Romano, plus ½ cup more for garnish

¼ cup dried bread crumbs

¼ cup chile powder

1 tablespoon cumin seeds,
  toasted and ground

1 teaspoon crushed red pepper flakes

1 tablespoon fine sea salt

½ cup blended oil for frying

16 corn tortillas, warmed

¾ cup thinly sliced scallions, for garnish

1. Make the *Chipotle* Salsa.

2. While the salsa is simmering, prepare the meatballs: In the jar of an electric blender, combine the chicken stock with the garlic, onion, and parsley; puree until smooth.

3. In a large bowl, combine the beef, pork, and veal with the eggs, *Cotija* cheese, bread crumbs, chile powder, cumin, red pepper flakes, and salt. Add the chicken stock mixture and gently mix until just combined. Form into walnut-sized meatballs.

4. Heat the oil in a large casserole, add the meatballs in batches, and brown evenly on all sides. Add the *Chipotle* Salsa, bring to a simmer, and cook until the meatballs are cooked through, about 15 minutes. Using a slotted spoon, spoon two meatballs onto each tortilla, and add the scallions, the remaining *Cotija* cheese, and the remaining chopped fresh parsley.

Isthmian-Style MEAT LOAF Tacos

YIELD: 10 TACOS

Meat loaf isn't only beloved in the United States. Throughout the Yucatán, the beautiful, strong Tehuana women sell Isthmian-style meat loaf at the stands or carts at markets and fiestas. The unique, tasty concoction is often eaten at room temperature. It makes a perfect sandwich or, in this case, taco. You can prepare the loaf 3 to 4 hours before baking, refrigerate it, and then return it to room temperature before cooking. Serve with Pico de Gallo.

2 thick slices bacon, cubed

2 ounces boiled ham, cubed

2 ounces smoked sausage, finely chopped

2 cloves garlic, minced

1 small white onion, finely chopped

1 cup plain dry bread crumbs

⅓ cup canned evaporated milk

½ pound ground beef

½ pound ground pork

1 large egg, lightly beaten

¼ cup blanched almonds,
    lightly toasted and coarsely chopped

½ (3½-ounce) can deviled ham

½ (2½-ounce) jar pimientos,
    drained and finely chopped

1 canned *chipotle en adobo*, minced

¼ cup pimiento-stuffed green olives,
    finely chopped

1½ tablespoons mayonnaise, not light variety

1½ tablespoons minced flat-leaf
    parsley leaves

1 tablespoon thinly sliced
    pickled *jalapeños*

½ tablespoon Dijon mustard

Pico de Gallo (page 39)

10 corn tortillas, warmed

¾ cup shredded lettuce, for garnish

½ cup crumbled *Cotija* cheese, for garnish

1. In a heavy, medium-sized skillet, combine the bacon with 2 tablespoons of water and cook over medium-high heat for 5 minutes, stirring frequently, until the water has evaporated and some of the fat has been rendered. With a slotted spoon, remove the bacon and set aside.

2. Strain the fat from the first pan (which will have a salty residue at the bottom) into a large skillet set over medium-high heat. Add the partly cooked bacon along with the ham and sausage. Cook until lightly browned, about 3 minutes, stirring frequently.

3. Using a slotted spoon or spatula, transfer the meat mixture to a bowl, leaving as much of the fat as possible in the pan. Discard all but about 2 tablespoons of the fat. Add the garlic and onion and sauté over medium-high heat until the onion is translucent, about 5 minutes, stirring often. Add to the meat mixture.

4. Meanwhile, in a medium-sized bowl, combine the bread crumbs and evaporated milk and let stand for 5 to 10 minutes to absorb the liquid while the meat mixture cools slightly.

5. Preheat the oven to 350 degrees.

6. In a large bowl, lightly mix the beef and pork with the soaked bread and beaten egg. Add the almonds, deviled ham, pimientos, *chipotles,* olives, mayonnaise, parsley, *jalapeños,* and mustard. Mix thoroughly with your hands. Pack the mixture firmly into a 9 x 5-inch loaf pan and bake until golden brown, about 1 hour.

7. Prepare the *Pico de Gallo,* if serving. Remove the meat loaf from the oven, let it rest for 15 minutes, then cut it into slices and serve hot or, as in the Isthmus, at room temperature on tortillas. Garnish with lettuce, *Pico de Gallo,* and *Cotija* cheese.

CHORIZO *and* POTATO
Filled Tacos

YIELD: 12 TACOS

Mexican chorizo, unlike the cured Spanish sausages of the same name, is sold raw, so it must be cooked through before using. When the seasoned pork is sautéed with onions and potatoes, it's a beloved and typical filling used in quesadillas and tacos throughout the country. Add Pico de Gallo *and* Cotija *cheese and these tacos can be enjoyed anytime from breakfast through dinner.*

Salsa Verde (page 33)

Kosher salt

1 pound russet potatoes,
    peeled and cut into ½-inch cubes

12 ounces Mexican chorizo sausage,
    casing removed (about 1½ cups)

½ cup finely chopped white onions

12 corn tortillas, warmed

½ cup crumbled *Cotija* cheese,
    for garnish

1 large avocado, preferably Hass variety,
    halved, seeded, peeled, and sliced,
    for garnish

1. Make the *Salsa Verde.*

2. In a large saucepan, bring 2 quarts of water to a boil. Add 2 teaspoons of salt and the potatoes and cook, covered, until just tender, 10 to 12 minutes. Drain.

3. In a large skillet over medium heat, add the sausage meat and sauté it along with the onions until the sausage is cooked through and onions are tender, about 10 minutes, breaking up the meat with a wooden spatula and stirring occasionally.

4. Drain and discard the excess fat. Add the potatoes to the skillet and cook until they begin to brown, stirring often. Keep warm.

5. Spoon the filling onto the tortillas, drizzle with *Salsa Verde,* and *Cotija* cheese, garnish with avocado slices, and serve.

Crispy PORK BELLY Tacos with Caramelized LADY APPLE Salsa

YIELD: 16 TACOS

With their succulent flesh and rich flavor, pork bellies are a decadent indulgence that have become quite popular lately, especially with foodies. In these tacos, I take them to an even more seductive level by serving them with Caramelized Lady Apple Salsa. The small green-and-red-tinged apples are mildly sweet with a tart note. I think you'll love this combination. Extra trimmings from the pork belly can be finely chopped and added to pinto beans for another taco filling.

2 cups apple cider vinegar

1 cup kosher salt

½ cup sugar

3 allspice berries

1 tablespoon black peppercorns

1 tablespoon whole coriander seeds

4 bay leaves, divided

1 (4-pound) piece uncooked pork belly, skin scored into cubes

2 quarts chicken stock

½ cup maple syrup

6 *chiles de árbol*

Caramelized Lady Apple Salsa *(recipe follows)*

Blended oil for frying

16 corn tortillas, warmed

CARAMELIZED LADY APPLE SALSA

1 cup sugar

½ cup heavy cream

1½ tablespoons unsalted butter

3 Lady apples, cored and quartered

1 *habañero* pepper, seeded and minced

1. In a large container, combine 2 quarts of cold water with the vinegar, salt, sugar, allspice, peppercorns, coriander, and two of the bay leaves. Soak the pork belly in the brine for 24 hours.

2. Preheat the oven to 325 degrees.

3. Remove the pork from the brine and lay it in a large, flat roasting pan. Add the chicken stock, maple syrup, *chiles de árbol,* and the remaining two bay leaves. Braise in the oven for 6 hours, spooning the liquid over the pork several times.

4. Remove the pork and transfer it to a sheet pan. Cover with a flat pan with several large, heavy cans on top (Number 10 cans work very well). Let the pork press for 8 hours in the refrigerator. Slice into 1-inch by ¼-inch-thick slices and reserve.

5. Make the Caramelized Lady Apple Salsa.

6. To serve: In a large, deep skillet, heat enough oil to measure 1½ inches deep until it's hot. Drop six or seven slices of pork belly into the oil at a time and fry until crisp, about 4 minutes. Season with kosher salt, layer in the tortillas, top with Caramelized Lady Apple Salsa, and serve.

Caramelized Lady Apple Salsa

In a medium saucepan, combine the sugar with ¼ cup of water; bring to a boil. Wash down any crystals on the sides of the pan with a wet pastry brush. Boil until the syrup is a rich amber color, about 6 minutes. Remove the pan from the heat and whisk in the cream (it will bubble up, so be careful) and butter. Stir in the apples and *habañero* and set aside.

BACON *Tacos with* *Chipotle* AIOLI

YIELD: 12 TACOS

Bacon—quite possibly humankind's greatest food invention—
can be consumed with anything. Tacos? Obviously!
For a great party appetizer, you can roll these up, secure with toothpicks, and deep-fry them.

Chipotle Aioli (page 47)

1 pound thick-sliced smoked bacon

1 medium white onion, finely diced

2 tablespoons honey

1 tablespoon *ancho* chile powder

½ teaspoon *chipotle* chile powder

Fine sea salt

¾ cup very thinly sliced iceberg lettuce

¾ cup thinly sliced radishes

1½ tablespoons blended oil

½ tablespoon red wine vinegar

Freshly ground black pepper

12 corn tortillas, warmed

1. Prepare the *Chipotle* Aioli.

2. In a large skillet, cook the bacon over medium heat until deep golden brown, turning often. Remove to paper towels to drain. Reserve the fat in the pan. Cut the bacon into 1-inch strips and transfer to a large bowl.

3. In the same pan, sauté the onion over medium heat until caramelized, 7 to 8 minutes, stirring often. Scrape into the bowl with the bacon and add the honey, *ancho* powder, and *chipotle* powder. Season to taste with salt.

4. In a bowl, toss the lettuce and radishes with the oil and vinegar and season with salt and pepper. Fill each tortilla with the bacon mixture. Spoon on some lettuce and radishes, drizzle with *Chipotle* Aioli, and serve two tacos per plate.

GOAT *Barbacoa* TACOS

YIELD: 16 TACOS

Throughout Mexico, barbacoa is an age-old tradition of marinating meats in an aromatic paste, wrapping them in avocado and/or banana leaves, and slowly roasting them for several hours or overnight in a deep pit in the ground. The technique evolved in pre-Hispanic times long before people had ovens. Almost every celebration includes barbacoa, and barbacoa specialists are hired.

The choice of meat varies throughout the country, including young pigs and lambs. In the north and central parts of the country, a young goat is preferred. Here it is rubbed with chile paste and cooked until the meat is fall-off-the-bone tender with subtle smoky flavors. Typically a whole animal is pit-roasted, and then the shredded barbacoa meat is served with chopped white onions, cilantro, and fresh chiles on the side.

3 *guajillo* chiles, stemmed and seeded

6 allspice berries

2 tablespoons dried oregano, preferably Mexican

1 teaspoon ground cumin

1 tablespoon fresh thyme leaves

3 cloves garlic

½ white onion, chopped

3 tablespoons apple cider vinegar

1 (3-pound) leg of goat

Fine sea salt and freshly ground black pepper

1 fresh or frozen banana leaf, cut into 12 x 12-inch squares

10 avocado leaves

16 corn tortillas, warmed

1 cup *each* chopped white onions, cilantro, and fresh chiles, for garnish

1. In a large saucepan, bring 1 quart of water to a boil. Toast the chiles on the griddle on each side until fragrant, about 2 minutes per side. Transfer to a bowl, cover with boiling water, and soak for 20 minutes. Drain and add them to the jar of an electric blender. Reserve the liquid.

2. Meanwhile, in a clean coffee or spice grinder, combine the allspice, oregano, and cumin; grind into a powder. Add this to the blender along with the thyme, garlic, onion, vinegar, and ½ cup of the soaking liquid. Puree into a smooth paste.

3. Score the goat leg into a diamond pattern, cutting it only ½-inch deep, and season it liberally with salt and pepper. Line a roasting pan with banana leaves, making sure they overlap the sides so they will cover the goat, then add the avocado leaves. Rub the chile paste all over the meat, lay it in the pan, and wrap the banana leaves around the goat. Cover the pan tightly with plastic wrap or aluminum foil and refrigerate overnight.

4. Heat the oven to 300 degrees. Remove the plastic or aluminum covering from the pan and discard.

5. Roast the goat until very tender, 4½ to 5 hours, turning once about halfway through. Drain the juices into a bowl and skim off the fat. Shred the meat. Pour the juices back over the meat and toss to combine.

6. Warm the corn tortillas. Divide the meat among the tortillas and serve two tacos per person. Pass the onions, cilantro, and chiles at the table.

VARIATIONS: Use a 3-pound leg of lamb or three or four meaty lamb or pork shanks.

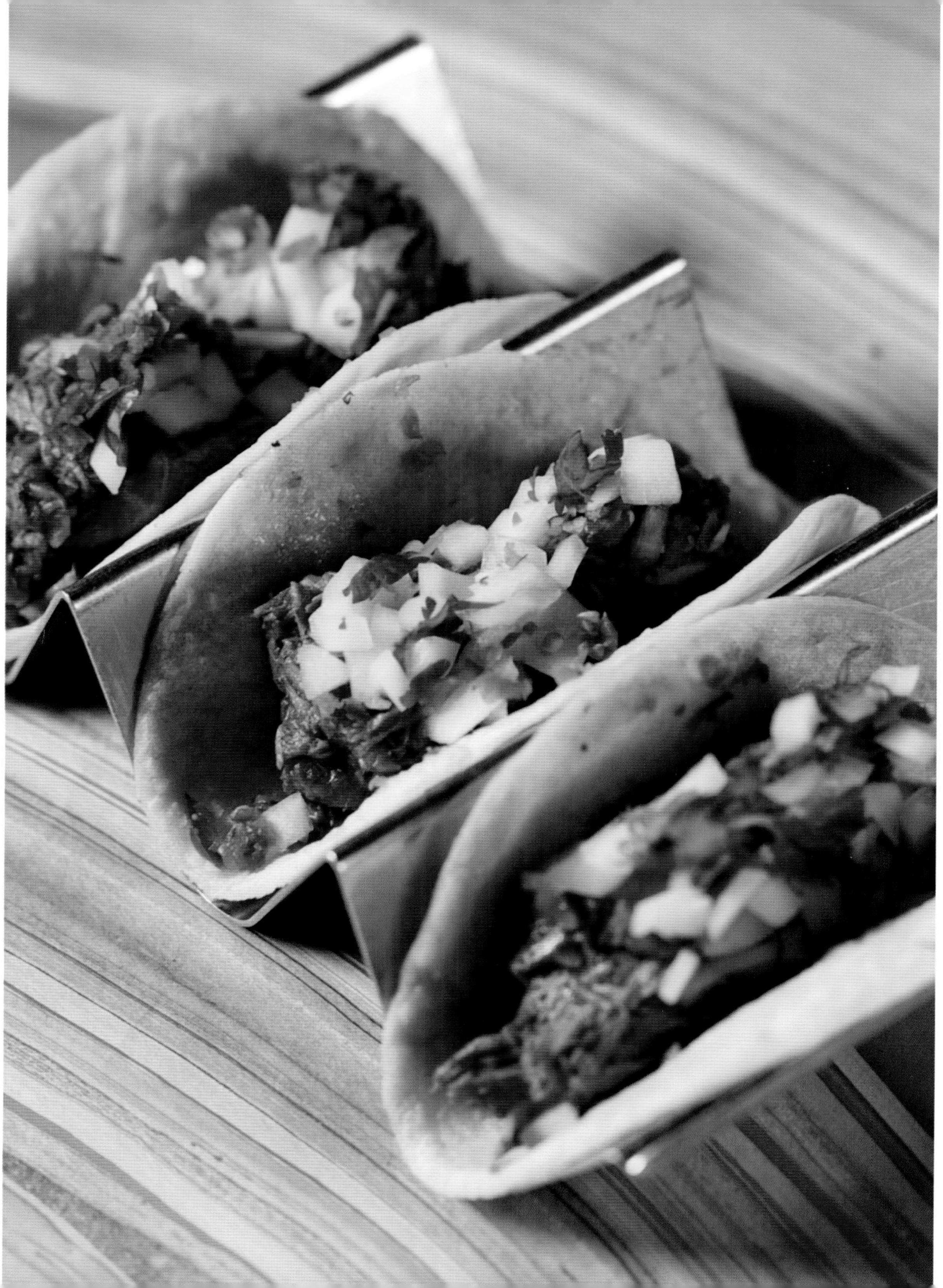

RABBIT *in* Adobo TACOS

YIELD: 16 TACOS

In pre-Hispanic Mexico, wild rabbits flourished and played an important culinary role. Today they are more often farmed and still readily available. I first tasted the meat at one of the string of roadside food stands along the Toluca Highway outside Mexico City.

The meat in these easily prepared tacos is delicate and takes well to the chiles and warm spices in the Abodo *Sauce. As with most tacos, I prefer that the meat isn't too finely shredded because it's more satisfying that way. The tacos are paired with Pickled Ramps, an underappreciated vegetable, also called a young leek. It tastes like a cross between onions and garlic. Substitute scallions for the ramps or serve with* Habañero *Pickled Red Onions (page 78).*

Cut-up rabbits are available at many butchers. If you buy whole rabbits, you could roast the loins and serve them roasted and sliced alongside this dish, if desired.

Hind- and front quarters from 5 rabbits

10 peppercorns

3 cloves garlic

3 bay leaves

1 white onion, coarsely chopped

Adobo Sauce *(recipe follows)*

Pickled Ramps *(recipe follows)*

Chiles Torreados *(recipe follows)*

16 corn tortillas, warmed

1. In a large saucepan, add the rabbits, peppercorns, garlic, bay leaves, and onion; pour in enough cold water to cover. Bring to a boil, reduce the heat, and simmer for 1 hour.

2. Meanwhile, prepare the *Adobo* Sauce and Pickled Ramps.

3. Cool the rabbits in the liquid. Remove them, pull the meat from the bones in large pieces, and reserve in a bowl. Reduce the broth by half, stir in the *Adobo* Sauce, and strain over the meat. Divide the meat among the tortillas and serve with the ramps and Chiles Torreados.

5 *pasilla* chiles, seeds and membranes removed

3 *ancho* chiles, seeds and membranes removed

3 cloves garlic, coarsely chopped

3 black peppercorns, crushed

3 sprigs fresh thyme

3 sprigs marjoram

3 whole cloves, crushed

½ stick cinnamon, preferably Mexican *canela*, crushed

¼ teaspoon cumin seeds, crushed

1 tablespoon white vinegar

PICKLED RAMPS

1 pound fresh ramps or scallions, trimmed and lightly blanched in salted water

¾ cup sugar

¾ cup rice vinegar

1 tablespoon kosher salt

½ teaspoon crushed red pepper

½ teaspoon *ancho* chile powder

CHILES TORREADOS

¼ cup olive oil

12 *serrano* chiles

12 Thai chiles

½ red onion, sliced

4 cloves garlic, thinly sliced

2–4 tablespoons Maggi sauce

Juice of 2 limes

Fine sea salt and freshly ground black pepper

Adobo Sauce

In a large bowl, soak the *pasilla* and *ancho* chiles in hot water to cover for 10 minutes. Using a slotted spoon, transfer them to the jar of an electric blender, add ½ cup of the chile rehydrating water, and puree. Add the garlic, peppercorns, thyme, marjoram, cloves, *canela,* cumin, and vinegar; puree until smooth.

Pickled Ramps

Put the ramps or scallions in a heatproof bowl. In a small saucepan, combine ¾ cup water with the sugar, vinegar, salt, red pepper, and chile powder. Bring to a boil. When the sugar dissolves, pour the liquid over the ramps, cover, and refrigerate overnight.

Chiles Torreados

YIELD: 2 CUPS

In taquerías, *roasted chiles are an indispensable staple for adding a spicy pick-me-up to tacos and just about anything else where you want a little heat. Although best eaten right away, once roasted and cooled, they can be refrigerated in a resealable plastic bag for a day.*

In a medium-sized heavy skillet, heat the oil over medium-high heat until hot. Add the chiles and sauté until they begin to blister, shaking the pan frequently, 5 to 8 minutes. Add the onion and stir until soft. Add the garlic and continue cooking until golden. Stir in the 2 tablespoons of Maggi and lime juice. Simmer to combine the flavors and to reduce the liquid slightly. Season to taste with salt and pepper, adding more Maggi sauce if desired.

SIDE DISHES

Elote de la Calle
(MEXICO CITY-STYLE STREET CORN)

YIELD: 8 SERVINGS

Everybody loves corn the way they serve it in Mexico City.
The seductive aroma of charred corn husks coming from street vendor carts
can be smelled almost anywhere in the center of town, or near most markets.
No matter where you're from or who you are, the grilled sweet corn
painted with butter and a little mayonnaise and salty Cotija *cheese will seduce you.*
Once the corn is cooked, if you cut it off the cob, it's called esquites.

8 ears corn, shucked

½ cup melted unsalted butter

½ cup mayonnaise, not light variety

½ cup grated *Cotija* cheese

1 tablespoon chile powder

2 limes, cut into wedges

1. Heat the grill, a large skillet, or a broiler over medium-high heat. Grill the corn until it's hot and lightly charred all over, using tongs to turn it.

2. Roll the ears in the melted butter and then spread with mayonnaise. Sprinkle with *Cotija* cheese and chile powder and serve with lime wedges.

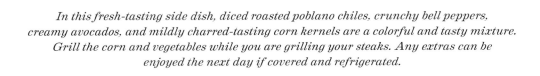

Avocado
CORN RELISH

YIELD: 4 CUPS

In this fresh-tasting side dish, diced roasted poblano chiles, crunchy bell peppers, creamy avocados, and mildly charred-tasting corn kernels are a colorful and tasty mixture. Grill the corn and vegetables while you are grilling your steaks. Any extras can be enjoyed the next day if covered and refrigerated.

5 ears corn, shucked and silk removed

4 green onions, light green and white parts, thinly sliced on the diagonal

4 *poblano* chiles, roasted, peeled, seeded, and cut into ¼-inch dice

1 large red bell pepper, seeds and membranes removed, cut into ¼-inch dice

2 avocados, preferably Hass variety

½ cup red wine vinegar

¼ cup olive oil

Fine sea salt and freshly ground black pepper

1. Heat a barbecue, grill, or broiler. Cook the corn until the kernels are tender and some are charred, about 5 minutes, turning a couple of times. Transfer the ears to a large mixing bowl and set aside to cool. When they're cool enough to handle, use a sharp paring knife to remove the kernels from the cob, transferring them to a large bowl along with the green onions, *poblano* chiles, and red pepper.

2. Peel, seed, and cut the avocados into ¼-inch dice. Add them to the corn along with the vinegar and olive oil. Mix well, season to taste with salt and pepper, and let the relish sit for 20 to 30 minutes to let the flavors blend. Serve at room temperature.

CHEF'S TIPS:

Use the green tops of scallions in salsa verde or salad dressings.

LEMON-BASIL
Rice

YIELD: 3 CUPS

Although basil or "albahaca" in spanish, is not typically associated with Mexican cuisine, it is used there both as a culinary and medicinal herb. This rice is refreshingly light and pairs well with any of the tacos in this book. It's also great with seafood and poultry dishes.

1½ tablespoons unsalted butter

½ small onion, finely chopped

1 cups long grain rice

dash turmeric

1½ teaspoons lemon zest, divided

1½ cups chicken stock

¼ teaspoon salt

1 tablespoons basil, cut in chiffonade

1½ teaspoons mint, cut in chiffonade

Fine sea salt

1. Melt the butter in a large sauce pan. Add the onions and saute until translucent. Stir in the rice and turmeric and cook until grains of rice are all coated and translucent. Add half of the lemon zest, the stock, and the salt.

2. Bring to a boil, cover, and simmer over low heat until tender, 20 to 25 minutes. Stir in the remaining lemon peel and herbs and serve.

My Refried BEANS

YIELD: 6–8 SERVINGS

Refried beans seem like a natural partner for tacos and are often included on platters with them. Too often, I find them boring. Hopefully that will not be your experience with my Dos Caminos version scented with the deep smoky flavor of avocado leaves and bacon.

When I was growing up in Denver, among the first foods my parents ordered for my sister and me were black bean tacos in a small storefront Mexican restaurant where we ate weekly. They're a simple, approachable food for any age. For a somewhat more grown-up version, check out Drunken Beans on page 229.

1 pound dry black or pinto beans

2 avocado leaves

2 slices bacon, cut crosswise
    into ½-inch strips

1 small white onion, diced

2 cloves garlic, minced

2 *jalapeños*, seeds and membranes
    removed if desired, minced

½ cup lard

Juice of 1 lime

Fine sea salt

Crumbled *Cotija* cheese,
    for garnish (optional)

1. Rinse the beans and soak overnight in a large pot of cold water. (If you don't have time to soak overnight, put the beans into a pot and cover with at least 2 inches of water. Bring to a boil, turn off the heat, cover, and let sit for 1 hour.) The following day, add fresh water and bring the pot of beans to a boil. Add the avocado leaves, turn the heat down, and simmer until tender, 2 to 3 hours.

2. In a large skillet, cook the bacon over medium-high heat until golden brown. Add the onion and sauté until golden, about 10 minutes. Stir in the garlic and *jalapeños* and cook for about 3 minutes, adding a little lard or bacon fat, if necessary, to keep the vegetables from sticking.

3. Drain the beans and reserve the cooking liquid. Scrape the onion mixture into a food processor along with about 2 cups of the cooked beans; puree. Combine the puree with the remaining beans.

4. In a large, heavy casserole, melt the lard over medium-high heat. Add the beans and fry for about 15 minutes, stirring frequently. Add the lime juice and season to taste with salt. If the mixture seems dry, add some leftover bean water until you reach the desired consistency. Serve topped with crumbled *Cotija* cheese, if desired.

Drunken BEANS

YIELD: 6–8 SERVINGS

These beans are My Refried Beans dressed up with bacon, chipotles en adobo, *mustard,
and the beer that gives them the name* frijoles borrachos. *They're a perfect side dish for any tacos,
or with warm tortillas and salsa as tacos in their own right.*

1 pound pinto beans, soaked according
   to package directions

1 pound thin-sliced bacon, cut crosswise
   into ½-inch pieces

2 carrots, finely diced

2 cloves garlic, minced

1 white onion, finely diced

1 stalk celery, finely diced

6 sprigs thyme, stemmed and
   finely chopped

Leaves from 1 bunch fresh oregano,
   preferably Mexican, finely chopped

1 tablespoon Dijon mustard

½ cup tomato paste

½ teaspoon ground allspice

1 canned *chipotle en adobo*, minced

2 (12-ounce) cans Mexican beer,
   preferably Tecate or Negra Modelo

Fine sea salt

In a large casserole, cook the beans in 4 quarts of water until just tender.
Drain and set aside. Cook the bacon in the same pan until done but not too
crispy. Add the carrots, garlic, onion, celery, thyme, oregano, mustard, tomato
paste, allspice, and *chipotle;* sauté until the vegetables are tender. Stir in the
beer, return the beans to the pot, and simmer for 10 minutes to combine the
flavors. Season to taste with salt.

Grilled NOPALES Salad

YIELD: 6–8 SERVINGS

Grilled cactus paddles, or nopales, *are a traditional Mexican side dish.*
When cooked over charcoal, they get a nice smoky taste, plus the heat firms up the texture.
Once they're tossed with tomatoes, cucumbers, onion, and Cotija *cheese, then seasoned with*
serrano *chiles, cilantro, and Cracked Black Pepper Oil, the paddles are a satisfying salad*
for any outdoor (or indoor) dining occasion.

1½ pounds fresh *nopales* cactus paddles

¾ cup extra-virgin olive oil, divided

1½ teaspoons fine sea salt, divided

4 heirloom tomatoes, cored and
    cut into ½-inch dice

2 cucumbers, peeled and
    cut into ½-inch dice

½ small red onion, cut into ¼-inch dice

2 medium *serrano* chiles, stemmed,
    seeded, and finely diced

1 cup chopped cilantro

½ cup finely grated *Cotija* cheese

½ cup red wine vinegar

1 teaspoon dried oregano,
    preferably Mexican

1 teaspoon freshly ground black pepper

6–8 red lettuce leaves

Cracked Black Pepper Oil *(recipe follows)*

1 avocado, preferably Hass variety,
    for garnish

CRACKED BLACK PEPPER OIL

¼ cup cracked black peppercorns

2 tablespoons extra-virgin olive oil

1 tablespoon red wine vinegar

1 teaspoon fine sea salt

1. To clean the cactus pads, use a large chef's knife and work parallel to each pad. Start at the top of each pad and pull the blade toward the stem, using a gentle sawing motion, to remove all of the thorns. Rinse well and pat dry.

2. Heat a barbecue or heavy ridged skillet until hot.

3. In a large bowl, toss the *nopales* with ¼ cup of the oil and ½ teaspoon of the salt. Lay the *nopales* on the grill and cook until they turn dark green with grill marks and black patches, turning once, 3 to 5 minutes total. Return them to the bowl to cool to room temperature. Cover and chill for 2 to 4 hours or overnight.

4. Slice the cactus into ½-inch pieces.

5. To serve, in a mixing bowl, combine the cactus, tomatoes, cucumbers, onions, chiles, cilantro, and cheese with the remaining ½ cup of oil, the vinegar, remaining 1 teaspoon of salt, the oregano, and the pepper. Toss well. Taste and adjust the seasonings, as necessary. Prepare the Cracked Black Pepper Oil.

6. Line eight salad plates with lettuce leaves. Peel, seed, and slice the avocado. Spoon on the salad, garnish with avocado, and sprinkle with Cracked Black Pepper Oil.

Cracked Black Pepper Oil

In a small bowl, combine the peppercorns, oil, vinegar, and salt. Stir before each use.

DESSERT
Tacos

Canela-Dusted DESSERT Tacos

YIELD: 8 TACOS

*Baked cinnamon-sugar-crusted taco shells filled with ice cream and fruit
make a fun finale to any dinner, Mexican or otherwise.
For added indulgence, spoon on warm chocolate sauce, chopped walnuts,
pecans, or peanuts, and whipped cream.*

¼ cup ground cinnamon,
  preferably Mexican *canela*

¼ cup fine sugar

Pinch fine sea salt

8 (6-inch or smaller) flour tortillas

2 tablespoons melted butter

Ice cream, flavor of your choice,
  softened slightly

Fresh fruit, such as berries, pineapple,
  and/or mango, again up to you

Optional toppings: warm chocolate sauce,
  chopped walnuts, pecans or peanuts,
  and whipped cream

1. Preheat the oven to 350 degrees. Tear eight 6-inch strips of aluminum foil or parchment paper and bend them into a V shape.

2. In a small bowl, combine the *canela,* sugar, and salt. Brush both sides of each tortilla with butter and sprinkle generously with cinnamon-sugar. Place each tortilla on a sheet pan and fold over the foil or parchment into a taco shell shape.

3. Bake until golden on one side, 8 to 10 minutes. Turn the tacos over and bake until the second side is golden, another 5 minutes.

4. Cool completely and then build dessert tacos by filling the shells with softened ice cream and adding your favorite toppings.

DARK CHOCOLATE *Tacos* *with* SOUR CHERRIES

YIELD: 8 TACOS

As a spectacular, if not traditional end to your meal, try these cocoa-scented taco shells filled with cherries, dark chocolate, mascarpone, and whipped cream. Place all the components in separate bowls and let everyone make their own for a fun, fiesta dish.

1 cup confectioners' sugar, divided equally

¼ cup all-purpose flour

3 tablespoons Dutch process cocoa powder

1 teaspoon cornstarch

¼ teaspoon fine sea salt

2 large egg whites, lightly beaten

1 teaspoon milk

¼ teaspoon pure vanilla extract

½ cup chopped bittersweet chocolate, plus shaved bittersweet chocolate, for garnish

1 teaspoon canola oil

¼ cup crushed almonds

½ cup heavy cream

½ cup mascarpone cheese

½ teaspoon ground cinnamon, preferably Mexican *canela*

2 teaspoons *añejo* tequila

½ cup finely chopped sour cherries

1. Preheat the oven to 400 degrees. Line a baking sheet with parchment. Using red or yellow food coloring, draw four 5-inch circles on the parchment. Suspend four thick wooden spoons crosswise over the edges of four deep bowls.

2. Sift together ½ cup of the confectioners' sugar with the flour, cocoa, cornstarch, and salt. Whisk in the egg whites, milk, and vanilla.

3. Spoon 1 tablespoon of batter onto each circle, spreading the batter to the edges of the circle using an offset spatula or the back of a spoon. Bake for 5 to 6 minutes, loosen the edges with the spatula or spoon, and carefully lift the circles off of the parchment. Working quickly, gently drape each taco over the suspended wooden spoons, gently shaping it into a taco shell. Cool completely. Repeat the procedure to make eight shells.

4. Combine the chopped chocolate and oil in a bowl and microwave on high power until the chocolate melts, about 1 minute, stirring after 30 seconds. Stir until smooth.

5. Spread about 1 teaspoon of the chocolate mixture on the top edges of the outside of both sides of the cooled shells, and sprinkle with about 1 teaspoon of the crushed almonds.

6. In a mixing bowl or stand mixer, whip the cream until firm. Do not overwhip. Using a rubber spatula, fold in the mascarpone along with the remaining ½ cup of sugar, *canela*, tequila, and sour cherries until well combined. Spoon ⅓ cup of the filling into each shell and garnish with shaved chocolate.

BEVERAGES

CHILACAYOTA
Agua Fresca

YIELD: 8–12 SERVINGS

Aguas frescas *are cool drinks made with water, fruit, and a sweetener (typically sugar)* *and are commonly served by Mexican street vendors in barrel-shaped clear jars called* vitroleros. *Meant to quench thirst, they are usually not overly sweet. This delicious pre-Columbian* agua fresca *comes from Oaxaca. It's made with* chilacayota, *a relative of the spaghetti squash, and is traditionally served with a scoop of cooling sorbet, such as lime.*

1 (3-pound) *chilacayota* squash
(most similar to spaghetti squash,
but any type may be used)

2 (6-ounce) cones *piloncillo*

2 (4-inch) sticks cinnamon,
preferably Mexican *canela*

1 pineapple, peeled, cored,
and cut into small dice

Grated zest of 1 lime

1. Split the squash in half, remove the seeds, and cut into medium-sized cubes. Put it in a large pan with 2 quarts of water, the *piloncillo*, and the cinnamon. Bring to a simmer over medium-low heat and cook until the squash is soft and can be easily removed.

2. Using a slotted spoon, remove the squash from the pan and remove the rind. Reserve the liquid. Return the squash to the pan with the liquid and, using a potato masher or handheld blender, mash the flesh until almost smooth.

3. Scrape the mixture into a bowl and cool to room temperature, then refrigerate until very cold. Add the pineapple and lime zest and stir until combined. Serve in tall glasses over ice.

PRICKLY PEAR
Lemonade

YIELD: 6 SERVINGS

Prickly pears grow on the opuntia cactus. Called tunas *in Spanish, they are eaten either chilled or at room temperature, and also made into candy and preserves. To enjoy the pears, you must carefully peel them and remove the many little spines. If you'd rather skip that step, prickly pear nectar is also available online. Four prickly pears yield about 1 cup of juice.*

4 prickly pears

¼ cup sugar

Juice of 6 lemons, plus slices for garnish

¼ teaspoon ground cinnamon, preferably Mexican *canela*

4 cups ice

1. Peel the prickly pears: Put them in a large bowl of cold water. Fold two or three sheets of paper towels together. Handling a pear on each end, lift it from the water and place it on the towels. Keeping the towels wrapped around most of the pear, use a small, sharp knife to slice along the length of one side, cutting just through the skin. Using the towels to protect your hands, peel the skin from the pear.

2. In the jar of an electric blender, puree the pears until smooth and pour through a fine strainer. Return the strained puree to the blender along with the sugar, lemon juice, *canela,* and ice; blend for 1 minute. Pour into tall glasses, garnish with lemon slices, and serve.

TAMARIND
Agua Fresca

YIELD: 8 SERVINGS

Sour tamarind is another popular flavor in Mexico.
Used for everything from medicine to candy, it was surely the inspiration for Sour Patch Kids.
The tangy and refreshing flavor is a nice counterbalance to spicy tacos.

16 large fresh tamarind pods
(about 1 pound total)

1 cup granulated sugar (or more to taste)

Ice

1. In a large pot, bring 1 quart of water to a boil over high heat. Add the tamarind pods and sugar and boil for 1 minute, stirring continuously. Transfer to a non-reactive bowl and steep for about 2 hours. This time may be as little as 1 hour for very fresh pods or up to 2½ hours for older pods. Use your hand or a spoon to break up the softened pods to free the pulp and the seeds.

2. Pour the mixture through a strainer, pressing on the solids to extract as much liquid as possible. Discard solid. Or, if desired, puree in an electric blender. Taste for strength and sweetness. If it is too strong, add water; if too tart, add more sugar. Cover and refrigerate until you're ready to serve. Stir before serving and pour over ice or serve cold without ice.

SWEET HIBISCUS
Punch

YIELD: 6 SERVINGS

When dried jamaica, *or "hibiscus," flowers are steeped in boiling water and sugar, then cooled, they become a beautiful garnet-colored punch that is a little bit sweet, a little bit tart, and super refreshing with a spicy taco.*

2 cups (2 ounces) dried *jamaica* flowers (hibiscus), sold in Latin grocers and online

¾ cup granulated sugar

1 (3-inch) piece fresh ginger, cut into ½-inch slices

Ice

1. In a large pot, bring 6 cups of water to a boil. Add the flowers, sugar, and ginger and stir continuously for 1 minute while the mixture boils and the sugar dissolves. Transfer to a stainless-steel or glass bowl and steep for 2 hours.

2. Pour the mixture through a strainer, pressing on the flower solids to extract as much liquid as possible. Taste for strength and sweetness. If it is too potent, add a little water; if it's too tart, add more sugar. Cover and refrigerate until chilled and time to serve. Serve over ice.

FROZEN *Margarita*

YIELD: 2 SERVINGS

Here are the basics to make a perfect frozen margarita.
There's absolutely no substitute for freshly squeezed lime juice in a margarita.
Keep Simple Syrup in the refrigerator for those emergency margaritas or
to sweeten iced tea or an agua fresca.

2 tablespoons Simple Syrup *(recipe follows)*

1 tablespoon Lime-Salt-Sugar *(recipe follows)*

1 cup crushed ice

3 ounces 100 percent agave silver tequila

¼ cup freshly squeezed lime juice

½–1 teaspoon orange liqueur

Lime wedges, for garnish

SIMPLE SYRUP

1 cup sugar

1 cup water

LIME-SALT-SUGAR

Zest of 1 lime

2 tablespoons kosher salt

2 tablespoons sugar

1. Make the Simple Syrup and Lime-Salt-Sugar.

2. In the jar of an electric blender, add the ice, tequila, lime juice, Simple Syrup, and orange liqueur. Cover and blend on high speed until smooth.

3. Pour the Lime-Salt-Sugar onto a plate. Press the rims of two chilled rocks glasses or wineglasses into the mixture to rim the edge. Strain the margarita into the glasses and serve garnished with lime wedges.

Simple Syrup

YIELD: 1½ CUPS

In a small saucepan, combine the sugar and water and cook over low heat, stirring, until the sugar dissolves. Remove and cool. Store extra syrup in a sealed container in the refrigerator for up to 1 month.

Lime-Salt-Sugar

YIELD: ¼ CUP

Combine the lime, salt, and sugar in a small blender or mini food chopper and blend until finely chopped.

SUMMER PEACH
Margarita

YIELD: 4 MARGARITAS

*When white tequila is shaken with lime juice, peach puree, and agave nectar
and set off by a piquant-sweet edge on the glass, it's a Mexican welcome to summer.
One hundred percent agave tequila is the sure way to avoid the hangover
you had in college from drinking too much mixto—you know the one: We all had it.*

Pink Peppercorn Blend to rim glasses
(recipe follows)

¼ lime

¾ cup 100 percent agave silver tequila

½ cup freshly squeezed lime juice

¼ cup fresh peach puree

2 tablespoons agave nectar

Ice

PINK PEPPERCORN BLEND

½ cup salt

½ cup sugar

¼ cup pink peppercorns

1. Make the Pink Peppercorn Blend and pour into a small, flat bowl. Run the lime along the top edge of four cocktail glasses and dip them into the mixture.

2. In a large mixing glass, combine the tequila, lime juice, peach puree, and agave nectar; shake 20 times. Add ice to the glasses and strain the margarita mixture into them. Serve at once.

Pink Peppercorn Blend

In a clean spice or coffee grinder, combine the salt, sugar, and peppercorns. Grind until fine.

Sangrita

YIELD: AT LEAST 12 SERVINGS

The name of this fiery Mexican drink means "little blood."
This spicy and addictive aperitif is served chilled alongside a shot of tequila for sipping.
Traditionally it's made with the juice of tomatoes, oranges, limes, and chiles.

2 cups tomato juice

1 cup freshly squeezed orange juice

¾ cup freshly squeezed grapefruit juice

½ cup freshly squeezed lime juice

2 tablespoons pomegranate molasses

1 tablespoon Maggi sauce

1 tablespoon Worcestershire sauce

1 tablespoon Valentina or other hot sauce

1 cup Tabasco sauce

1 tablespoon kosher salt

1 bottle premium tequila,
   to serve as shots on the side

1. In a large container, mix together the tomato, orange, grapefruit, and lime juices.

2. Add the pomegranate molasses, Maggi, Worcestershire, Valentina, and Tabasco sauces along with the salt. Stir to blend.

3. Refrigerate or serve on ice with a shot of tequila on the side.

BLUE POM
Margarita

YIELD: 2 SERVINGS

This margarita, made with blueberry-pomegranate juice, is not only bright and fresh tasting, but also a beautiful color. It is one of the most popular margaritas at Dos Caminos.

Ice

3 ounces 100 percent agave silver tequila

¼ cup freshly squeezed lime juice

2 tablespoons agave nectar

1 tablespoon blueberry-pomegranate juice

Fresh blueberries, for garnish

1. Fill a cocktail shaker with ice. Add the tequila, lime juice, agave nectar, and blueberry- pomegranate juice. Cover and shake until mixed and chilled, about 30 seconds.

2. Strain the margarita into two glasses over fresh ice. Garnish with fresh blueberries.

MICHELADA

YIELD: 1 SERVING

More sophisticated than simply a beer with a squeeze of lime, and one of the most popular ways to quench even the biggest thirst, the Michelada has as many variations as there are bartenders. However, all rely on salty, sweet, and umami *tastes. This is mine.*

Coarse salt, for rimming the edge
of the glass

Ice

½ lime

1 splash pineapple juice

2 dashes Mexican hot sauce

2 dashes Maggi sauce or
Worcestershire sauce

1 bottle Mexican beer, dark or light
according to taste

1. Dip the rim of a highball or pilsner glass in the salt.

2. Fill the glass with ice. Squeeze in the lime, add the pineapple juice, hot sauce, and Maggi, and pour the beer over the ice.

CHILES
Explained

Chiles pictured, from left:
(first row) Pasilla Negro, Brown Chipotle, Bird (Thai), Mulato
(second row) Serrano, Jalapeno, Chili de Arbol, Ancho
(third row) Cascabel, Guijillo, Poblano, Habenero

CHILES, EXPLAINED ◆-◆-◆-◆-◆-◆-◆-◆-◆-◆-◆-◆-◆-◆-◆-◆-◆-◆

Fresh and dried chiles bring an enormous variety of flavors to Mexican dishes. While working with them isn't complicated, for those of you who haven't used them before, I have some suggestions.

First, remember to wear gloves! Touching chiles and then your eyes can be really irritating. Also, while I often leave the seeds and membranes in chiles, these are the hottest parts of the peppers. Remove them if you prefer to diminish the heat.

When buying dried chiles, look for those that are unbroken with a deep color and that smell fresh. Store them in airtight containers (preferably separated and labeled) in a cool, dry spot out of the sun. Plastic bags are vulnerable to pests. Dried chiles will remain viable for at least 6 months.

Fresh:

***Jalapeño* chiles** (above) take their name from Jalapa, the capital of Veracruz, Mexico. The smooth, dark green chiles turns bright red when ripe. They range from mildly hot to very hot. *Jalapeños* generally are about 2 inches long, have rounded tips, and are quite popular because they're so easily seeded (the seeds and veins are very hot). In their dried form, *jalapeños* are known as *chipotles*.

***Habañero* chiles** are among the hottest chile peppers. They are native to the Caribbean, the Yucatán, and the north coast of South America. Small and lantern-shaped, *habañeros* range from light green to bright orange when ripe. Generally they are used for sauces in both fresh and dried form.

***Poblano* chiles** (below) are dark green with a mild, rich flavor. Generally about 4 to 5 inches long, they taper from top to bottom in a triangular shape. *Poblanos* are found in central Mexico, though they are now grown in the U.S. Southwest as well. In their dried state they're known as *ancho* or *mulato* chiles.

Serrano chiles are about 1½ inches long. The slightly pointed chile has a very hot, savory flavor. As it matures, its green skin turns bright red, then yellow. *Serranos* can be used fresh or cooked in various dishes such as guacamole and salsa. The dried *serrano* chile is called *chile seco* and is generally used in sauces.

Dried:

Ancho chiles are ripened and dried *poblano* chiles. Triangular in shape—broad at the top and tapered to a blunt tip at the bottom—and deep red in color with wrinkled, shiny skin, they average 4½ inches in length and 3 inches across the top. Most are mild with a fruity, slightly acid flavor, but, depending on where they were grown, the soil, the amount of water received during the growing season, and the climate of the land, some may be quite hot. While they're similar in size and shape to *mulato* chiles, you can tell the difference by holding them up to a light: *Anchos* will have a reddish hue, and *mulatos* will be chocolate brown.

Chiles de árbol ripen to bright red and are then dried. This smooth-skinned, slender chile tapers to a sharp point and typically measures about 3 inches long and ³/₈-inch wide. Thin-fleshed and very, very hot, *árbol* chiles develop a sharp flavor when lightly toasted. You find them often used for hot table sauces, for frying whole and adding to dishes, like a pot of beans, or ground into a powder as part of a recipe or as a condiment for sliced fruit, cucumbers, or jicama.

Cascabel chiles are a deep reddish color and round in shape with a smooth polished surface. The name means "small bell," and the chiles rattle when shaken. *Cascabels* are available throughout Mexico and most often used in table sauces. They are more

frequently incorporated into dishes in central-western and northern parts of the country. They are pleasantly hot and nutty and measure on average about 1¼ inches wide and 1 inch long. When rehydrated, these chiles become quite fleshy.

Chipotle chiles are ripened, smoke-dried *jalapeños*. The name is derived from the Nahuatl words for "chile" (*chil*) and "smoke" (*pectli*). There are two varieties of *chipotles*: the *mora*, which is mulberry-colored, and the larger *meco*, which is tobacco brown (it is grown red and dries to that color). The average chipotle is 2½ inches long and about 1 inch wide, is very spicy, and becomes quite fleshy when rehydrated. The versatile chipotle is used for pickling, as well as for flavoring soups, sauces, fish, and meat dishes. Canned *chipotles en adobo* are commonly used in Mexican cooking.

Costeño chiles are grown in Northern Oaxaca and Coastal Guerrero, as the name implies, as well as the Mixteca Baja, where they are used almost exclusively. The chiles average about 3½ inches in length and ½ - inch wide, tapering to a pointed tip; they're a rich bronzy red color with a thin, almost transparent, shiny skin. Most often they are dried, though sometimes they may be sold when ripe, but still green. *Costeños* range in sharpness from very hot to pleasantly mild. A less popular bronzy yellow variety from the same area is usually used toasted and ground with garlic, salt, and water for a rustic table sauce, sometimes with tomatoes added.

Guajillo chiles (opposite page), along with *ancho* chiles are among the most commonly used chiles in Mexico. The name means "big pod." Inexpensive and readily available, the chiles are reddish in color with a tough, opaque, shiny, smooth skin. Shaped like an elongated triangle with narrow shoulders tapering to

and stews.

Mulato chiles get their name from their brown color. The plant is like a *poblano* with slightly different genes that affect the color and the taste of the fruit. When mature, these chiles are a very dark green that deepens to a rich brown as they ripen. *Mulatos* range from mild to fairly hot and have a sweetish taste that, along with their color, makes them perfectly suitable for mole *poblano*. When rehydrated, they are fleshy and have a mild, faint chocolate taste.

Pasilla chiles are the dried form of *chilaca* chiles. The name simply means "large"; they are also known as *negro* chiles in some parts of Mexico. *Pasillas* are long and narrow with blunt or slightly pointed ends and shiny black, puckered skin and vertical ridges. On average they are about 6 inches long and 1 inch wide. *Pasillas* range from hot to fairly hot and when rehydrated have a sharp but rich flavor. Also very versatile, *pasillas* can be used in table sauces and moles, or stuffed, fried whole, or cut into strips for a garnish.

Pasilla de Oaxaca chiles are unique and delicious chiles used almost exclusively in Oaxaca and in a limited part of neighboring Puebla. They are grown in small quantities in isolated valleys in rugged terrain. Usually left to ripen on the plant and then smoked in rustic conditions, they tend to be fruity and smoky, but also extremely hot. Like the *pasilla*, the chile has a shiny, wrinkled skin, and pointed tip; it varies in length and is fleshy when rehydrated. This rare chile is expensive, and usually sold by count of 100 rather than by weight.

a pointed tip, an average-sized *guajillo* measures 5 inches long and 1¼ inches across the top. They have a crisp, sharp flavor that varies from fairly hot to very hot. When rehydrated, *guajillos* are fleshy inside, but their skin remains tough, so sauces made with them are usually strained. *Guajillos* are versatile and used for table sauces, enchiladas, *adobos* (seasoning pastes),

GLOSSARY

GLOSSARY

With the increased popularity of Mexican and other ethnic foods across America, most of these ingredients are available in Latin grocery stores, in local supermarkets, or from online purveyors.

Achiote paste is made by grinding annatto seeds, spices, garlic, and vinegar or lime juice together until smooth. It is popular in the Yucatán Peninsula.

Adobo is a tangy combination of chiles, garlic, and vinegar along with tomatoes and spices that is used as a marinade or sauce to season meat or poultry dishes.

Avocados are extremely popular in Mexican cooking. The California Hass variety with its dark green, bumpy skin is more flavorful and less watery.

Avocado leaves have an anise-like flavor and are used dried and fresh to season stocks, soups, and sauces.

Banana leaves are quite pliant and used to wrap meat dishes, like *barbacoa*, especially in and around Oaxaca. They are sold frozen at specialty markets.

Canela, or Mexican cinnamon sticks (at right), are softer in texture and milder tasting than American cinnamon that comes from cassia bark. They're also easier to grind.

Chile powder is made from ground dried chile peppers. It can be made with a blend of several chiles or from just one variety, such as *ancho* or *chipotle*, and can range from mild to fiery hot.

Chipotles en adobo are smoked *jalapeños* packed in *adobo* sauce and canned. They are now also available already pureed and canned.

Chorizo in Mexico, unlike Spanish or Portuguese sausage with the same name, is always purchased raw; remove the casing before you cook with it. The

pork meat is seasoned with ground red chiles, paprika, and sometimes *achiote*, which give it its characteristic reddish color.

Cilantro is among the most commonly used herbs in Mexican cuisine. Both the stem and leaves are used. The plant was introduced into Mexico by Spanish conquerors; the seeds of the plant are called "coriander."

Crema is Mexican sour cream. I prefer Media brand, by Nestlé. It is readily available online. If you can't find it, you can mix American sour cream thinned with heavy cream to a smoother consistency, or substitute crème fraîche or Greek yogurt in most recipes.

Epazote is an important Mexican culinary herb that tastes like a mix of mint, basil, and oregano. The long, jagged, pointy leaves become more assertive as the plant ages, so younger leaves are preferable. *Epazote* is a popular addition to bean dishes because it is said to reduce flatulence. Use oregano as a substitute.

Huitlacoche (or *cuitlacoche*) is a fungus that grows on ears of Mexican corn. During the growing season, the smoky-sweet flavored delicacy, also called "Mexican truffle" or "Mexican caviar," is frozen or canned for export if it is not eaten fresh.

Jamaica flowers are the beautiful fuchsia-colored blossoms of the hibiscus tree that are dried and used in beverages like *agua de jamaica*, sorbets, and granitas.

Jicama is a crunchy slightly sweet-tasting tuber known as Mexican potato. It has light brown skin and almost white flesh. To peel jicama, use a sharp paring knife to pull off the fibrous skin in sheets. It is easier than using a vegetable scraper.

Lard has long been the fat of choice in Mexican cuisine, where it imparts a distinctive flavor to traditional preparations like *masa* for tamales. Americans now realize that lard makes pastry flaky and that it has less saturated fat than butter.

Maggi sauce is a condiment, much like Worcestershire sauce, that's frequently used in Mexican marinades, stews, and sauces. It is very salty, so just a dash is all you need.

Masa harina is cornmeal or corn flour typically sold in 1-kilo (2.2-pound) bags. It's used for tamales and tortillas. There are different grinds, from fine to coarse, as well as different colors, including blue. The term *masa* refers to any type of "dough." I use Maseca brand.

Mexican oregano is widely used in the cuisine of Mexico. It is usually purchased dried or in flakes and is slightly sweeter and a little stronger than Greek, Italian, or Sicilian varieties. It is readily available online.

Nopales are the paddles from young cactus plants. The needles must be removed before they are marinated and grilled or used in other preparations. (See page 230.)

Onions used in Mexican cooking are usually white, but the yellow variety is acceptable.

Piloncillo (below) is unrefined Mexican dark brown sugar that is sold in solid cone shapes with flattened tops. The cones are sold in sizes from under an ounce to more than half a pound. While it's firmer in texture than American brown sugar, the two can be used interchangeably. However, *piloncillo* must be chopped with a serrated knife before using.

Pimentón de la Vera is Spanish smoked paprika that is available in sweet (mild) and hot varieties.

Plantains are similar to bananas but starchier and less sweet. A plantain is ripe when it is black and soft. They are readily available today in supermarkets.

Queso blanco is a creamy, soft, and mild white cheese generally made from whole cow's milk. It is fresh rather than aged. It does not melt well but softens when heated and is used for frying. It is similar to *queso fresco*..

Queso Chihuahua is made from cow's milk in the state of Chihuahua. One of the most popular Mexican cheeses, it is high in butterfat with a flavor similar to mild cheddar. When aged, it becomes tangy tasting. It's typically used in *chiles rellenos*, Mexican-style fondue, and quesadillas. Good-quality Muenster or medium cheddar can be used in its place.

Queso Cotija is an aged, white, salty, crumbly cheese named for the town in Michoacán where it was first made. When heated, it softens but doesn't actually melt. It is similar to feta when fresh, or to Parmesan when aged. You can substitute feta, Romano, or Parmesan.

Queso fresco, as the name implies, is fresh, unaged cow's-milk cheese that is produced all over Mexico. Other local names include *queso de metate*, *queso molido*, and *queso ranchero*. The cheese is used fresh, as a table cheese, crumbled as a topping, or as a stuffing for chiles or quesadillas because it melts well. It has a pleasant acidity and creaminess.

Queso Menonita is a mild, semisoft cheese made from either pasteurized or raw cow's milk, It is similar in taste to Monterey Jack. In Northern Mexico, several Mennonite communities proc**Quesillo Oaxaca** is a whole-milk cow's cheese from the Central Valley of Oaxaca that is creamy-colored with a pleasantly acidic bite. Typically the cheese is sold as wound balls. It melts well and can be shredded and used to top appetizers or as a filling for quesadillas or *chiles rellenos*.

Queso Requesón is similar to ricotta with a mild, somewhat sweet flavor. White, with a soft, moist texture, it is used in salads, tacos, cooked foods, and dessert.

Salt is important in cooking, but if it is iodized, I think it imparts a metallic taste. I suggest using either kosher or fine or coarse sea salt, as indicated by the recipe.

Tacos are usually made with fresh corn tortillas folded in half and filled with any combination of meat, cheese, vegetables, and condiments including tomatoes, lettuce, and salsa.

Tamarind paste is the acidic-sweet-tasting pulp surrounding the seeds of the tamarind pod. It has many uses, including *agua fresca* and Tamarind Braised Short Ribs (page 183).

Tomatillos, members of the gooseberry family, resemble small green tomatoes with a papery husk covering that is removed before using. They're slightly tart but very flavorful. They are used in many sauces, especially *salsa verde*.

Tortillas are thin, circular disks of unleavened dough made of *masa* for corn tortillas or *harina* for flour tortillas. They are the most important item in Mexican cuisine.

Valentina hot sauce is my favorite brand of hot sauce, although there are plenty of other brands out there including Cholula, another great brand.

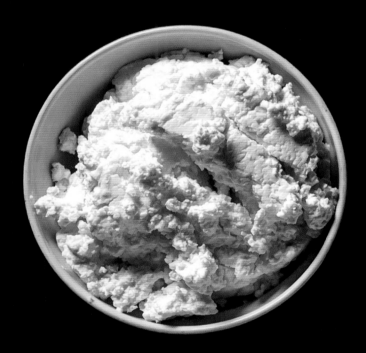
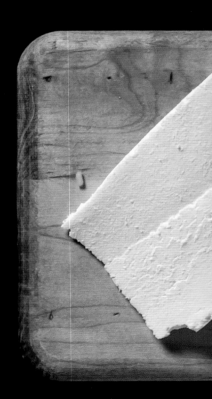

Mexican cheeses, from left to right:
Cotija, Queso Fresco, Fresco, Menonita, Oaxaca

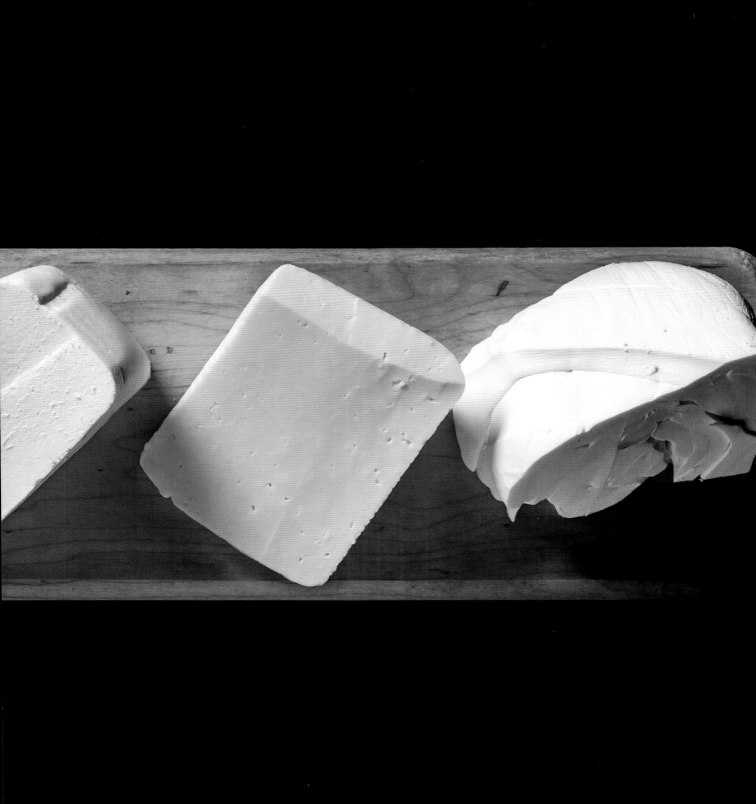

DOS CAMINOS

BEER $6

PACIFICO	SOL
BOHEMIA	NEGRA MODELO
TECATE	MODELO ESPECIAL
CORONA	CORONA LIGHT
BUD LIGHT	BUDWEISER
DOS EQUIS (LAGER & AMBER)	
BLUE POINT TOASTED LAGER	
$7 - SAM ADAMS & STELLA ARTOIS	

BLANCO

CORAZON	10
EL TESORO	11
CASA NOBLE	11
TRAGO	13
LUNA SUEÑO	13
CORZO	14
CUERVO RESERVA	16
MILAGRO SELECT	19
GRAN PATRON PLATINUM	45

REPOSADO

SIEMBRA AZUL	11
CABO WABO	11
SAUZA TRES GENERACIONES	13
EL MAYOR	13
TRAGO	14
MAESTRO DOBEL	16
FRIDA KAHLO	19
TEZON	
MILAGRO SELECT	

AÑEJO

SAUZA CONMEMORATIVO	11
PURA SANGRE	14
CORAZON	16
EL DIAMANTE CIELO	16
SAN MATIAS GRAN RESERVA	19
DON JULIO 1942	35
PARTIDA ELEGANTE	65
PATRON BURDEOS	110
1800 COLECCION	200

extra añejo

ACKNOWLEDGMENTS

As most cookbook authors discover, it takes far more than a passionate chef to write a book that others will want to read, find useful, and enjoy owning. *Dos Caminos Tacos* was just such a collaborative effort among me and many friends, colleagues, and family members. Throughout my career, my mother, Charlene, and father, Russ, along with my sister, Holly, have always been enthusiastic and proud supporters. And although my immediate family isn't around the corner, Frida and Diego, my faithful and affectionate dachshunds, eagerly await my return home and never fail to put a smile on my face even after (or especially after) a long, stressful day.

My sincerest gratitude goes to Stephen Hanson, the founder and president of BR Guest Hospitality, who continues to encourage me to expand my horizons and let me write this, my second book for Dos Caminos. Donna Rodriguez, our vice president of marketing, was a huge supporter from the conception of the book to its completion.

Dos Caminos's executive sous-chef Joy Strang was invaluable in methodically testing the recipes and making the food photo-ready. Her commitment to this project was beyond extraordinary. Executive chef David Chiavaroli also helped test the recipes, especially in the beginning.

I'm forever grateful to Cara Gambardella and Wendy Schlazer, my counterparts in the front-of-the-house operations at Dos Caminos; Dos Caminos's executive chefs: David Chiavaroli on Park Avenue, Roberto Hernandez in the Meatpacking District, Brian Mannett in SoHo, Michael Penaranda on Third Avenue, Elizabeth Barlow in Fort Lauderdale, Florida, and Ryan Ebbs in Atlantic City, New Jersey; and the staff in all of the kitchens and dining rooms, for your unfailing professionalism and friendship. You inspire me every day. I'm also grateful to all of the support staff in the corporate offices at BR Guest Hospitality, as well as my fellow chefs and managers who willingly have shared ideas, friendship, and advice through the years.

Additionally, I am so grateful to my current and past mentors: Chris Giarraputo, Brett Reichler, Normand Laprise, Andy D'Amico, Gary Robins, Mary Sue Milliken, Susan Feniger, and Ricardo Zurita Munoz.

I also love to read about food. The books that have influenced me recently are Hank Shaw's *Hunt, Gather, Cook* for the dedication to honest food. His book and wonderful blog make me think every day about where my food comes from. Maricel E. Presilla, *The New Taste of Chocolate: A Cultural and Natural History of Cacao with Recipes*, which goes beyond anything I have read on Mexico's most beloved native delicacy. And I always go back to my Betty Crocker cookbook to dream. The illustrations and photos are of my childhood, and I have a deep nostalgia for that wonderful time in my life.

Thanks to Noah Fecks, our extraordinarily talented photographer, for his lively and creative pictures, and Ann Treistman, our editor at The Countryman Press/ W. W. Norton, for ardently championing this project.

And finally, thanks to Joanna Pruess, my collaborator. I'm not a writer by any means but a chef who is passionate about Mexican food and who loves to share with food lovers. This book would not have been possible without Joanna by my side to help me translate my thoughts to paper. Thank you for everything.

—*Ivy Stark*

Note: Page references in *italics* indicate recipe photographs.

INDEX